Women Leaders

Women Leaders

The Power of Working Abroad

Sapna Welsh and Caroline Kersten

BEP BUSINESS EXPERT PRESS

Women Leaders: The Power of Working Abroad

Copyright © Business Expert Press, LLC, 2019.

First published in 2019 by
Business Expert Press, LLC
222 East 46th Street, New York, NY 10017
www.businessexpertpress.com

ISBN-13: 978-1-94944-397-4 (paperback)
ISBN-13: 978-1-94944-398-1 (e-book)

Business Expert Press Human Resource Management and Organizational Behavior Collection

Collection ISSN: 1946-5637 (print)
Collection ISSN: 1946-5645 (electronic)

Cover and interior design by Exeter Premedia Services Private Ltd., Chennai, India

First edition: 2019

10 9 8 7 6 5 4 3 2 1

Printed in the United States of America.

Abstract

This book explores how to attract, develop, and retain more talented women in leadership pipelines by accelerating their development through a powerful approach—working and living abroad. This book delves into the topic of women's leadership at a crucial time when organizations are increasingly international, the business environment is volatile, and a leadership crisis is growing worldwide. To meet the resulting demands, organizations need talented men and women leaders to execute strategy, deliver top service, and offer innovative thinking to drive results.

Section 1 reviews the growing leadership shortage concerning CEOs around the world, and builds a narrative for gender diverse leadership pipelines to address this problem. We discuss the value of expatriate assignments for career development, and how women can pursue these opportunities. We consider potential barriers to get such roles and introduce methods to dismantle them.

Section 2 is dedicated to understanding global leadership competencies which facilitate peak performance, accelerate assimilation into a new environment, and create a smoother transition into an international role. We review a standard global leadership competency model and then take a deep dive into the four competencies that are more pronounced among women in senior-level expatriate roles (WiSER): self-awareness, conscious imbalance, active career management, and operating outside your comfort zone.

Section 3 is dedicated to other important factors to effectively transition into an international role. Preparing for transition includes learning about cultural dimensions in order to decipher cultural diversity and determine when to adapt or not to adapt. We conclude the book with how to be impactful during the first 90 days in a new international role. This is a time of high visibility fraught with challenges. Strategically networking and communicating will enable one to effectively meet the challenges and establish credibility.

Keywords

career management; cross-cultural communication; diversity; expatriation; gender bias; glass border; glass ceiling; global leadership competencies; international assignment; international leadership; men as allies; mentors and sponsors; psychological safety; talent development; women leaders

Contents

Endorsements

"Women Leaders - The Power of Working Abroad is filled with ground breaking research, meaningful stories, and hands on exercises for women who want to enrich their professional journey by leveraging international work experience."

—Prof. Holger Ernst, PhD, Chair for Technology and Innovation Management, WHU, Otto Beisheim School of Management

"In *Women Leaders - The Power of Working Abroad* the authors, Caroline and Sapna, make a convincing argument for having more females participate in the global work process. They have gathered up-to-date materials for going beyond anecdotal evidence. Females bring something to the party that is unique to them, making the expatriate job more fulfilling. Bravo!"

—Fons Trompenaars, author of Riding the Waves of Culture
Cross-cultural expert, ranked in the Thinkers50 listing, and voted one of the top 20 HR Most Influential International Thinkers by HR Magazine.

"Finally - here is a book that puts the professional woman in focus and takes you through the challenges from both the personal, family and business perspective. A must read for any woman who has an interest in an international career. *Women Leaders - The Power of Working Abroad* is a great read - packed with great stories and tons of practical advice. Read, enjoy and conquer the world."

—Deanna Rasmussen, Global Mobility Manager NEME, APAC & India - Siemens Gamesa

"This book brings together useful and important information for female expatriates."

—Neelie Kroes, Non executive board member Salesforce, Rijksmuseum; Advisory Board Uber. *Former Vice President of the European Commission. Has made the Forbes' - The World's 100 Most Powerful Women list multiple times in the past decade.*

"*Women Leaders - The Power of Working Abroad* represents a tremendous contribution, and should be required reading for all students of international business. Female students need it to help optimize their expectations and preparation for their future role in our global economy. Male students, as future managers, need it to help them overcome an *unfounded* yet persistent prejudice against women serving as expatriates—a prejudice that is not only unfair to women but also renders uninformed organizations at a great disadvantage in the global war for talent."

—Dr. Charles M. Vance, author of *Managing a Global Workforce* and management professor at Loyola Marymount University

Introduction

Who you are today is a reflection of your experience. Who you will become tomorrow will depend on the experiences you are yet to choose.
—Authors Caroline Kersten and Sapna Welsh

Business is moving at lightning speed, becoming ever more global, requiring both stellar leadership and great adaptability to succeed. Consider this, of the companies listed on the Fortune 500 in 1955, only 61 (or 12 percent) remained in 2014. That means 88 percent of the original companies either went bankrupt, merged, or fell from grace due to decreased total revenues. About 50 years ago, the life expectancy of a firm in the Fortune 500 was around 75 years. Today, it's less than 15 years and declining (Levensaler 2016). Companies do not simply decline because they fail to strive for better, but because leadership may not be asking the right questions, vetting diverse perspectives and solutions, or is reluctant to implement those solutions. A current dilemma, however, that executives are keenly aware of is the lack of leaders to drive business imperatives. Despite a 39 percent increase in corporate spending on leadership development in the US alone, there is a growing leadership crisis (HBR 2014). This is the moment in time when organizations can evolve and thrive by asking themselves what they can do to attract and retain top talent to build robust leadership pipelines. Top talent by definition is inclusive of both men and women. However, women are still lagging behind. After reaching an all-time high of 32 in 2017, the number of female Fortune 500 Chief Officers has slid back down to 24 resulting in a one-year decline of 25 percent (Fortune 2018).

We train and coach diverse talent to prepare them for next level roles. We also work with organizations to grow and diversify their leadership pipelines, with a cultivated specialty in increasing the number of women leaders. Diversifying leadership pipelines will require the commitment of both men and women in organizations. Leadership development among diverse groups is the red thread that runs throughout our careers from being on the ground floor for the launch on the Women's Initiative at

Deloitte, to leading the inclusion strategy for JPMC T&O, as well as speaking multiple languages and working and residing in numerous nations. In 2013, we released research on the crest of women rising into leadership roles. Inspired by hundreds of interviews with impressive women leaders, we published our research on how women could continue to advance their careers through the non-traditional approach of expatriation. In 2017, we introduced the Gender Parity Spotlight™ (GPS) survey to help spotlight and measure what women in their respective organizations see as facilitating and impeding factors to their upward career transition. In 2018, we released GPS research on barriers stopping women from taking next level roles.

In response to swelling organizational demands to grow and diversify talent pipelines, we decided to write this book to re-energize the effort to support aspiring women accelerate their leadership trajectory by leveraging the most powerful development tool—working and living abroad (Hogan 2009).

Research Methodology

The foundation of this book lies in extensive primary and secondary research. A special mention to Prof. Dr. Anja Karlshaus, Dr. Charles M. Vance, and Shawn Garrett for reviewing the script, and Dr. Zachary Kalinoski for his superior data analysis and reporting skills.

In order to determine some of the most prevalent barriers women face when moving into leadership roles, we used the GPS survey. See Appendix A for additional details. The GPS provides a measurable way for organizations to create a customized, targeted strategy to retain and grow their talented women. Barriers are measured across three dimensions:

- Individual: Barriers that women impose upon themselves. Do self-limiting beliefs and behavior hold women back from pursuing leadership roles?
- Organizational: Barriers that women perceive the organization is imposing. Do women perceive that their employer is well equipped to develop and promote women to leadership roles?

- Transitional: Barriers to women's transition readiness. Do women believe they are prepared for a transition into a next level role?

Each dimension captures a grouping of barriers stopping women from moving into leadership roles. The higher the barriers are, the greater the risk of women leaving the leadership track or leaving the organization altogether. The goal is for organizations to have a low risk score, which indicates that they have few barriers preventing women from moving into leadership. In November 2017, we used the GPS to compile new research based on the responses of over 1,000 career women in 24 industry sectors in multiple countries to better understand what barriers women perceive are standing in their way to a next level role.

For our research on expatriate experience, we interviewed women in senior-level expatriate roles (WiSER) from all corners of the globe who shared their own strategies to overcome challenges, and succeed, when working abroad. For the purpose of this book, the term expatriate is defined as individuals who establish their residence in the territory of another country for a temporary period that is, or is expected to be, of at least 12 months and a maximum of five years per assignment, having previously been resident in another country. We have intentionally refrained from further defining the term expatriate and have elected not to include points such as benefits packages, retirement packages, guaranteed or non-guaranteed employment upon return, and so forth. This decision was based on our determination that these types of variables are not related to leadership development. The intent of the research was to identify shared behaviors for success in an international assignment. The women we interviewed fell into the categories of C-level, executive, or emerging executive. We validated their seniority based on various criteria, including (but not limited to) title, span of control (number of staff and geographical responsibility), salary, and budget managed. The sample group represented a broad range of age, nationality, marital status, and industry sectors. Among the finalized sample group, we interviewed 62 women representing 150 expatriate assignments. See Appendix B for additional details.

These interviews, along with the subsequent analysis, constitute the most comprehensive research on professional expatriate women to date. The WiSER we interviewed are amazing women who held challenging roles across the globe. We cannot but admire their commitment, their professionalism, and their achievements. A few of their career highlights include:

- "Top 25 Most Influential Female Engineers in Germany" in 2012.
- Most senior woman in Bayer and the first female expatriate in the C-Suite in this organization.
- First woman to lead her organization's office in Egypt, in all of the 50 years that CARE had been there.
- Set up the first Africa regional recruitment office for World Vision Africa.
- Led the IPO for Amazon.com.
- Expatriate in the Arctic Circle.
- Global Chair of the Board of Fair Trade International.

Throughout this book, leaders share, with refreshing candor, their professional and personal stories including challenges they were forced to overcome, and the steps they took to manage their career. These stories reflect both self-initiated and organization induced expatriate experiences.

SECTION I

CHAPTER 1

Calling All Leaders!— The Growing Leadership Shortage

Women hold up half the sky.

—*Mao Tse Tung*

My mother would say, "With your skills, with your languages, you can become the personal assistant of a CEO," but she couldn't quite imagine that I would become the CEO myself.

—*WiSER Flavia*

To achieve goals in a complex business environment, organizations need the best men and women leaders. Leaders are those who practice the art of motivating a group of people to act toward achieving a common goal. The title of leader is earned by demonstrating important qualities associated with leadership today. Peter Economy, an authority in the field of leadership, listed the following qualities of today's best leadership: decisiveness, awareness, focus, accountability, empathy, confidence, optimism, honesty, and inspiration (Economy 2014). Leadership characteristics can be demonstrated at any level in your career. When organizations consider building leadership pipelines, they actively include talent at all levels who demonstrate leadership qualities in order to prepare them for next level roles.

Today's business landscape includes considerations of political instability, terrorism, global recession, and concerns of technology replacing jobs. Yet, the top two concerns that have kept CEOs up at night across the globe for three years and running are developing the next generation of leaders and attracting and retaining new talent. Without talented leaders at the helm, who is left to execute strategy, deliver top service, and identify and build out new markets (Conference Board 2018)?

By 2030, the global talent shortage could reach 85.2 million people—costing companies trillions of dollars in lost economic opportunity (McLaren 2018). Headlines border on fear mongering:

- Financial and business services will be 10.7 million
  workers short.
- Supply chain staff shortages may reach global crisis by 2020.
- World Bank sounds alarm on logistics worker shortage.
- In tech alone, the United States could lose out on
  $162 billion worth of revenues annually unless it
  finds more high-tech workers.

To create solid, sustainable leadership pipelines, organizations align and prepare their current workforce to their future business goals and needs (also known as workforce planning). It is imperative to include diverse talent in workforce planning efforts, resulting in more robust leadership pipelines. One way to create diverse pipelines, is to look beyond the current composition of leaders and include more women. The topic of female leadership is highly pertinent in this critical period of the rise of women's influence in the world, a threatening shortage of talent and leaders, and intensified globalization. The commitment of both men and women in organizations is key to diversifying leadership pipelines.

Why Do We Need More Women Leaders?—The Business Imperative

How can the stresses of the leadership challenge be lightened? How can projected economic growth and competitive advantage be sustained? We recommend that organizations "fish where there are fish"—that is, harness educated, capable, available yet untapped talent (namely women) and remove barriers preventing them from moving into leadership. In looking at the Fortune 500, only 5 percent of CEOs are women as of 2018 (Zarya 2018). Only when both women and men lead at the top together, organizations can achieve their highest level of performance.

On top of alleviating the leadership crisis, diversifying talent pipelines has some very positive "side effects"—namely, superior organizational results. Organizations that have positive and inclusive corporate cultures and effective talent management strategies achieve better financial results and do better in times of uncertainty:

- Increasing the percentage of women in senior roles from zero to 30 percent will generate 15 percent more profit (Curtin 2017).
- Innovation intensity which results in more patents, is on average 20 percent higher among companies with women in top management roles. (Blumberg 2018).
- Having female senior leaders creates less gender discrimination in recruitment, promotion, and retention. That gives a company a better chance of hiring and keeping the most qualified people (Noland 2016).
- A large female presence is associated with higher status. Fortune's "most admired" companies have twice as many women at the senior management level than less reputable companies (Blumberg 2018).
- More than 70 percent of purchasing decisions are made by women. Diverse leadership teams have a greater chance of connecting with the buyer and show stronger customer orientation. Inclusive companies create positive brand image in large and growing diverse target markets. "Leading organizations will embrace diversity as a way to win 'the next billion customers'—those who are in untapped geographies or have been traditionally underserved" (Donaldson 2017).

While researchers are attempting to specifically discern why companies with more women at the top are performing better, here are a few known data points. One, to reap the rewards of diversity in leadership, organizations will want to focus on having women in top positions (Lorenzo 2017). Two, it is important to have a supportive set of policies, such as child care, education, and non-discrimination, which allows women to maintain their careers in a relatively undisruptive manner. For example, research from Pew Research Center showed that "mandated maternity leave did not correlate to increased female leadership, but more robust *paternity* leave did" (Pew Social Trends 2015). Three, men and women have different leadership strengths that complement each other contributing to improved leadership performance. Groups like NASA have found that even space missions go better when the crew consists of both males and females (Credit Suisse 2012). Similarly, a field experiment with teams of student entrepreneurs that had to start up, sell stock for, and actually run 43 real companies with the goal of maximizing profit and shareholders' value showed that gender-balanced teams outperformed both male-dominated and female-dominated teams (Hoogendoorn 2013).

How Do We Get More Women Leaders?—The Fast Track

In order to accelerate talented women into leadership, working and living abroad is a key development opportunity that more women are recognizing and taking advantage of. Courtney Ellis-Jones of the Forum for Expatriate Management noted the increasing trend for young professional women to go on foreign assignments as part of their career development (Roberts 2016). As per the 2016 Global Mobility Trends report, the percentage of women expatriates has steadily increased to 25 percent (BGRS 2016). Many of these women are under 30, doing it solo, or taking their partners with them. Despite the fact that nearly 70 percent of global mobility leaders indicated they use international assignments to develop their pipeline of future leaders, only 22 percent reported that they were actively trying to increase the number of female expats (PriceWaterhouse-Coopers 2016). In an effort to support more women to pursue working and living abroad, we will share strategies women can use to secure an international role and prepare for success on the job in order to rapidly develop their professional capabilities.

Paths to an International Assignment

Working and living abroad is distinctly different than visiting a country or commuting for work. Women in senior-level expatriate roles (WiSER) shared that, although preparation is important, all the preparation in the world can only take you so far. WiSER Jolanda said: "That's what I realized when I came over to Switzerland really not knowing the Swiss at all. I mean I've been skiing on holidays but … that doesn't mean you get to know the Swiss … You prepare yourself that it will be different, but you can never prepare for how different." WiSER Anna agreed that it is impossible to prepare yourself for all of the challenges involved in an expatriate assignment. "You do have different working environments … That was something I did find quite difficult," she said. "But I can't see how you can possibly prepare for that. You know it is something that you can only really experience by being there."

While it is impossible to "know" the unknown, tools such as the Internet, social media sites, websites that are dedicated to international relocation, and relevant books and blogs can help you boost your level of awareness and preparedness. Cultural classes can be extremely beneficial and help you understand how and why "business as usual" is different in your host country. Equipped with such knowledge, you will have a deeper understanding of why people behave the way they do in your host country. The key to success is not to know everything, but rather to face new challenges and opportunities with an open mind and confidence. Regardless of the type of assignment you may pursue, WiSER Heidi provided the following insight, "When you make a move like that, everything is exciting, vibrant, and sparkling, with renewed enthusiasm and excitement. I was very receptive to the move, and therefore people were very receptive to me. Excitement is infectious."

There are two primary paths to obtain an expatriate opportunity: either you are sent abroad by the organization you're working for—the organization induced expatriation (OIE), or you find a job in another country on your own—the self-initiated expatriation (SIE). Regardless of the path you select, it is necessary to demonstrate high performance and leadership skills in order to be considered for an international role (Brookfield 2012, p. 16). If you are interested in an expatriate role, it is important to develop a brand that reflects what you can bring to such a role and share your interest broadly. Download the Women Leaders Toolkit from the BEP publishing website for additional tools and resources. Whether you pursue an international opportunity through your employer or on your own, there will be distinct differences, and associated pros and cons (Table 1.1).

Table 1.1 Characteristics of organization-induced expatriation (OIE) and self-initiated expatriation (SIE)

	Organization induced expatriation (OIE)	**Self-initiated expatriation (SIE)**
Categories of assignment	• Talent development focus— work abroad for the purpose of getting a project or opportunity to develop yourself • Expatriate assignment—traditional, long-term (average two–five years) • Relocation to another country for work • Permanent/one-way transfers—relocation to another country • Short term assignment—up to 12 months • Intra-regional role—covering various countries within a region • Global Nomad—move from nation to nation, typically without returning to home country	• Staffing focus—hired to work abroad to meet a staffing need. • Permanent/one-way transfers—relocation to another country • Short-term stay—example, study abroad • Intra-regional role—covering various countries within a region • Global Nomad—move from nation to nation, typically without returning to home country
Being considered as a candidate	• Expatriate selection processes often poorly structured • Less accessible to women because of home country barriers • Companies are looking for alternatives to traditional expatriate roles	• Challenging to identify appropriate roles • Good way to overcome home country barriers
Moment of expatriation	• Indefinite period of time to be considered for such roles	• Timelines can be determined and managed
Regulatory environment	• Organization sponsors work permits, visas, tax equalization, and so on	• Have to be self-managed • Host country employer has to justify international hire
Level of support	• Greater security and organizational support	• Limited security and organizational support • Relocation for international work, as well as the return home have to be self-managed

Cultural adaptation	• Takes more conscious effort because traditional expatriates often work and live in expat circles	• More natural adaptation due to intensive interaction with host country nationals
Networking	• Active career management within the organization (known territory)	• Active networking in the intended host country (unknown territory)
Mobility	• Build career within the organization	• Mobile across organizations

Sources: Vance, McNulty and Chauderlot (2011); Hu Mo and Xia Jian-Ming (2010) and Mercer (2018).

The Benefits of Working and Living Abroad

Many questions will undoubtedly cross your mind when considering an expatriate role, with a central question being: "What do I stand to gain, or lose, from living abroad and working in a different culture?" The WiSER overwhelmingly indicated that they believe that expatriate opportunities help individuals grow, both personally and professionally (Figure 1.1). This sentiment is partially attributed to the fact that they increased their network and developed competencies and skills at a hastened pace, in a unique way that enriched growth, outlook, and personal life as well. Significantly, the majority of the WiSER we interviewed were married and/or had children. Those with children suggested their international assignment provided their family with a valuable experience that could not have been achieved any other way. Although the WiSER shared with us some of the challenges they faced, they ultimately agreed that the benefits outweighed any negatives.

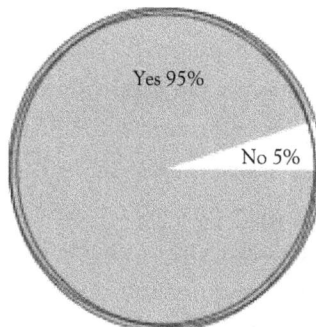

Yes 95%

No 5%

Figure 1.1 Was your career enhanced by your international assignment?

The Society for Human Resources Management (SHRM) conducted a similar survey and asked assignees, "How far was your international assignment helpful for your personal and professional growth?" (SHRM 2004). More than 90 percent of the respondents indicated their assignment had been very helpful for their professional growth, especially in terms of global awareness, cultural workplace savvy, leadership skills, and career development. In addition, assignees indicated that leadership skills and managerial skills could be developed more efficiently during long-term expatriate assignments, as opposed to shorter assignments. As far as personal growth was concerned, more than 95 percent of respondents rated global assignments as very helpful, especially in increasing or creating cultural awareness, strengthening the ability to adapt and increasing flexibility.

If you were to ask people what their most valuable asset is, more often than not, the most common response would be a material item, most likely their house. In all actuality, a professional's most valuable asset is their earning potential. International experience is an undeniably positive investment to grow one's earning potential as it increases skills, capabilities, and experience. During expatriate assignments, the WiSER acquired and/or enhanced skills, knowledge, and competencies that were valued upon return, and their experience made them more valuable to their own organization, while also attracting the interest of other organizations. In short, it enhanced their careers. Let's take a look at the five most frequently mentioned benefits of working and living abroad.

Accelerated Learning and Development

Working and living abroad offers a unique, accelerated learning experience that is difficult to find otherwise. The current pervasive philosophy around learning and leadership development is the 70-20-10 model developed by Lombardo and Eichinger in 2000. The model demonstrates that 70 percent of learning is provided through the use of challenging assignments and on-the-job experience. An expatriate role is an ideal opportunity to develop leadership capabilities because it offers many challenging work experiences, exposure to new thinking and approaches, constant training on the job and an opportunity to build relationships and expand networks around the world. This is the essence of the new leadership profile.

"The fact is, you will be absorbing a lot of information very quickly." WiSER Andrea said. "It's about being able to learn something new and understand something differently than you did before." She indicated that gaining a broad range of experience was the true value of working abroad. WiSER Andrea added that, if she had remained in her native Brazil, she would have needed to work at many different companies to accumulate the variety of experiences she gained through one international assignment. "This [fact] that you deal with different people in their own environment ... that's very rich," she said. "It's different than if you always stay in your own country." WiSER Hermie agreed. "It's a great learning opportunity, both personally and professionally," she said. "It's a quantum leap in learning. What you would learn over many years, you learn in a very short span of time." Meanwhile, WiSER Julie Anne revealed that she had unique experiences in Latin America she couldn't have gained through a domestic assignment. "In Latin America the organization is smaller, and it's a growing operation, and [that] is when there's a lot of what we call white space or opportunities that haven't been tapped yet," she explained.

> So, even as a middle management person you're making decisions that would ordinarily ... be made by people two levels higher than you. The learning is so much richer in that kind of environment where there's a lot of freedom and flexibility to make decisions and make an immediate impact on your business.

Competitive Advantage

For many of the WiSER, the competitive advantage of an international role was obvious. Acquiring and/or refining skills and competencies during an international assignment is not only beneficial within your current organization, it also positions you as an appealing candidate for other organizations. This is confirmed by a study where expatriates were asked what the career impact was of their international assignment: 40 percent said that they were promoted faster than their peers, 36 percent indicated that it was easier to obtain new positions in the organization, and 16 percent indicated they changed employers more often, thanks to their improved competitive position (Brookfield 2012, p. 16). WiSER Anne noted that, within two years of her return to the United States, she was headhunted for the job of president and CEO of a global non-profit organization. She recalled: "They were looking for someone who actually had a lot of hands-on experience overseas—and I had almost 20 years of it—and someone who would help run a very large organization, and I had done that with my chief of staff job for a year and a half."

Leadership Skills

Working and living abroad cultivates leadership skills by testing leadership capabilities in many ways. The popular theories around situational leadership, as developed by leadership gurus Paul Hersey and Ken Blanchard, state that there is no single best style of leadership. Rather, successful leaders are able to adapt their style to the task, person, or situation at hand. When operating in a foreign environment situational leadership takes on a whole new dimension. "I believe that an international assignment can accelerate my career because not everybody has had that experience," said WiSER Allyson. "It has taught me valuable skills especially on the communication front, how to motivate and lead different types of individuals from vastly different backgrounds." The next generation of leaders will be required to possess a global mindset because they will be managing an increasingly diverse workforce. The characteristics required for global leadership are learned, and they can be developed rapidly in international roles. Working and living abroad, you will encounter different ways of thinking, communicating, collaborating, leading, and accomplishing small to large goals, just to name a few. This forces you to reflect on your own ways of doing and being. "I believe an international assignment can accelerate or enrich your career because it makes you a better person," WiSER Stacy indicated. "I think it will do wonders to enhance your career. It will make you more open and more aware of your own assumptions and how at times they may be false." Intimately experiencing new cultures will lead to a greater understanding and appreciation for different viewpoints and approaches resulting in improved methods of collaboration and issue resolution. "An international assignment is absolutely worthwhile," said WiSER Nina.

> It will lead to better cooperation and problem solving that you cannot solve in just one nation. It will lead to a different kind of society because people who are internationally skilled ... and have been exposed to an experience in another country, have this certain openness that I think is needed. We have this vision of the global citizen ... maybe somebody who can, without forgetting about his own background, nationality, or ethnic identity ... still be open. I would go as far as saying that this may lead to a more peaceful world.

Financial Rewards

Expatriation packages can be very comprehensive, dealing with many aspects related to your move. There are many resources available to assist you with the logistics of your move abroad, including relocation firms. The issues you may need to contend with may include negotiating your expatriate contract, solving tax issues, or finding a house. Download the Women Leaders Toolkit from the BEP Publishing website for additional tools and resources.

If you receive a comprehensive expatriate package, you may feel as though you have hit the jackpot. After all, when is the last time someone paid for your rent or your car? Bear in mind that as an expatriate, you may incur costs that you typically wouldn't have. When WiSER Alicia moved to Germany, she found "the biggest challenge we had was, quite frankly, the cash flow. You had to have such a huge cash outlay for everything because this country does not operate on credit as you do in the US." Whether you are self-initiating expatriation or supported by your organization, be aware of hidden costs and cost of living differentials.

Personal Growth

As the WiSER agreed, there are many benefits to an international assignment. "Absolutely, international experience benefited my career," said WiSER Nina. "But the greatest benefit was for my personality. I became a much more self-confident, fulfilled person." WiSER Annes shared: "I definitely took advantage of living far away. I learned that I can live anywhere in the world," she revealed.

> I learned that people across the world are very helpful and receptive, and caring, and that it depends on how you approach them. I realize that the world is a really small place but a really interesting place. I have learned a lot and I really have loved the journey.

As per a recent HSBC report, 52 percent of expats report having a better overall quality of life (BGRS 2016). "Personally, it gave me the opportunity to meet some needs and motivations that I had—that have really made me feel … much more content," said WiSER Diane. "And as a person I feel more satisfied with my life." Additionally, when you are living in a different country—with different norms, values, and ways of doing things—you start appreciating many of the things you associate with your native country. WiSER Carrie. "It definitely shaped our lives. We know people now. We know cultures now. We know a lot of things we never would have known before—and your view of the world, it does change, and it also helps you truly appreciate what you have at home." She added that she has learned to recognize many of the assets of her native country. "Canada is a fantastic country," she said. "I always thought it was and I do even more so now." Being farther away from home can also strengthen relationships with family and friends. An old proverb says, "Absence makes the heart grow fonder," and this is very true when you live abroad. As WiSER Andrea discovered. "The positive thing is that some of the relationships actually grew stronger, with my parents, with my sisters, because we don't have daily issues," she said. Moreover, with modern technology it is relatively easy to maintain and nurture contacts at home. As WiSER Pauline shared: "The international, expatriate experience is a fantastic one, simply because it just completely changes your lens on the world."

We focus on an in-depth examination of global leadership behaviors that contribute to the success of female expatriate leaders. We have uncovered that WiSER share an additional four competencies that help women excel in their expatriate assignment: Self-awareness; Conscious imbalance; Active career management; Operating outside your comfort zone.

As a woman considering an international job, developing these four global competencies will lead to greater success in an international role. Specifically, it will position expatriate women to:

- Achieve peak performance
- Accelerate assimilation into your new environment
- Facilitate a smoother transition

It's a Wrap

In today's business environment, leadership's top concern continues to be attracting, retaining, and developing talented leaders. In the face of a growing leadership shortage, the solution lies in diversifying talent pipelines. Specifically, women who represent approximately 50 percent of the potential workforce are a resource to be targeted. There are many benefits to including more women in the leadership ranks and addressing the leadership crisis is foremost among them. Expatriate experience is an underutilized approach to accelerate development and get ambitious, talented women in the talent pipelines at a higher and faster rate. There are two main ways to expatriate, self-initiated or organization induced. Regardless of the path, the journey is career enhancing. Working and living abroad provides intense learning and development of leadership skills, and a global mindset. There is a long term professional competitive advantage, as well as financial rewards. Notably, expatriate opportunities help individuals grow, both personally and professionally.

CHAPTER 2

Don't Let Anything Stop You

The question isn't who's going to let me; it's who is going to stop me.
—Ayn Rand

When you are deciding to do or not do something, remember that a few years out, you are going to look back. At that point, never ever be in a situation where you say, "What if?"
—WiSER Anuradha

Have you wondered how to:

- Propel your career?
- Explore the world?
- Learn another language?
- Travel and visit people you know around the world?
- Have 1,000's of professional connections that you actually know?
- Position your experience more individually?
- Boost your financial prospects?
- Lead the world of tomorrow?

It is all possible through working and living abroad—the most powerful leadership development tool. History is filled with stories of bold explorers, who challenged existing notions and endured hardship to discover new lands and new treasures. Exploring the world is challenging and requires a large dose of courage and vision and a dash of madness. You may find what you are looking for, and you are bound to find the unimaginable.

A powerful approach to increase the percentage of women in leadership is to fast-track their career development through working and living abroad. This is most effective when done in combination with traditional approaches, such as hiring greater percentages of young women; train, develop, coach and promote them into senior roles; and institute policies that support them in these roles.

Research from McKinsey has shown that women are as ambitious as men (McKinsey 2016). Notably, 89 percent of women who voluntarily leave their jobs, for various reasons, want to return to work. Despite their ambition, however, it remains difficult for women to realize their leadership goals. It is important to put a common misconception—that women are not interested in leadership or expatriate roles—to rest. Research dating as far back as the 80's has shown that men and women are equally interested in international assignments, and that there was no difference between single and married people (Catalyst 2000). Women are not only interested in expatriate roles but are willing to work around the glass border by self-initiating expatriation approximately 30 percent more frequently than men (Vance, McNulty, and Chauderlot 2011). Again, over one-fourth of WiSER self-initiated their international careers in order to expedite their opportunity to progress their careers and work abroad. The growing trend around self-initiated expatriation tells us that women are interested in international assignments and are willing to take considerable risks and "go it alone" in order to secure such opportunities.

While women represent over half the available talent pool, many organizations struggle to retain and grow talented women. Organizations lose 40 percent of their female talent between entry level and VP. In the face of leaking talent pipelines and stagnating percentages of women moving into leadership and international roles, we went a step further to identify barriers preventing women from accessing such roles in order to dismantle them.

Barriers to Advancing Professionally

Barriers slowing or stopping women from moving into leadership roles are real. Domestic female leaders face the glass ceiling in their efforts to move up, the "unseen, yet unbreachable barrier that keeps ... women from rising to the upper rungs of the corporate ladder, regardless of their qualifications or achievements" (Federal Glass Ceiling Commission 1995, p. 4). In their efforts to move "out," female expatriate leaders face an additional barrier, the "glass border," that prevents women from securing expatriate assignments.

Individual Barriers

Individual barriers can appear as self-limiting beliefs or behaviors that women impose on themselves. These perceived challenges influence how women weigh the pros and cons associated with career progression and the influence of external factors on career progression. Some common individual barriers are: (1) not asking for what they need; (2) not feeling confident unless they are 100 percent prepared; and (3) not promoting their achievements. As WiSER Maxine notes, "women don't call enough attention to their own achievements. While it would be nice to think that your accomplishments would be recognized by your superiors without you having to call attention to them, this is not the way it works." Why does a woman shy away from getting her voice in the room? Why does she avoid advocating for what she believes to be inequitable compensation or rewards? Why does she hold back her potential contributions? At a macro level, many of these challenges take root because it is far more challenging to speak up and be heard when you are an outsider.

Another individual barrier that is frequently cited is the lack of work-life balance that may come with a leadership role. As per the GPS survey results, however, 55 percent of respondents do not feel guilty if they have less than "complete" balance. Furthermore, 68 percent shared they do not let pressure from family and friends dictate professional choices and 60 percent shared they have supportive relationships in their professional life. Although the potential lack of work-life balance continues to be an ongoing challenge, our research did not find that it was among the most dominant self-imposed barriers.

Organizational Barriers

Organizational barriers are challenges women perceive the organization is imposing. Whether the organization recognizes these barriers or not, the women's perception of them can lead to disengagement and to women leaving the leadership pipeline. Three top organizational barriers include (1) implicit bias in recruitment and promotion; (2) linear career pathing; and (3) lack of role models.

First, it remains difficult to recruit people from diverse groups and to leverage the associated benefits. Implicit biases affect how we assess others' performance and capabilities. For example, researchers at the Ohio State University set out to test the relationship between academic success and job market success. They sent out over 2,000 job applications to entry level positions around the United States using dummy resumes. The results found that women who were academically successful had the lowest success rate, especially when they majored in traditionally male-dominated fields, such as mathematics. The highest achieving men were called back 16 percent of the time, men with the worst grades 11.7 percent of the time, compared to only 9 percent of the highest achieving women. The study's author suggests that employers value competence and commitment among male applicants, but value likability among female applicants (Shen 2018).

Data relative to both the glass ceiling and the glass border demonstrate that in most countries of the world, women still face biases and prejudices that men do not have to face. For example, studies show that both men and women think men are more competent and hirable than women, even when they have identical qualifications (Dewar 2018). Women have to prove themselves more than men do to be noticed, and to get credited for their achievements. Even when women prove themselves, men get promoted and expatriated more often and earlier in their careers. In our most recent research women perceive the biases in the performance evaluation system as a major barrier. In fact, 58 percent believe they are not paid the same as their male peers for similar performance in the same role. Additionally, 43 percent believe women are not routinely considered for promotions. The GPS survey results revealed that 45 percent of the women feel they need more education and qualifications than male peers to be considered for promotion.

So, what can be done to combat this bias against diverse groups? First, define clear selection criteria for recruitment or promotion purposes, and for performance evaluations. For example, there is a widespread myth that "women don't want these roles" and often times are not even asked if they are interested in certain opportunities. It is simply assumend they don't. By defining clear standards beforehand, the risk of bias slipping in is considerably reduced.

> Even as companies say they want to develop the careers of their female high-potential employees through mentorship programs or leadership workshops, many are still not encouraging them to take on high-profile global roles. Some firms assume that family responsibilities or obligations are obstacles holding back women in their careers, but not men in theirs,

says Emrich, vice president at Catalyst, a global non-profit organization that promotes women in the workplace (Dizik 2016).

Second, the majority of career pathing models are linear, resulting in sourcing candidates around their early 30's for management as well as international opportunities. This model is more disadvantageous to women because this decade of life often coincides with family planning considerations. If the traditional linear career pathing is used, it is critical for organizations to offer strong support, such as comprehensive family support policies, to retain talented women in talent pipelines (Cohen 2017). Another opportunity is for organizations to seek talent at various intervals and various levels in the organization. The WiSER recommend overcoming this barrier by sharing the value you contribute while calling attention to your unique needs and considering the demands involved in the role.

Third, few women hold senior-level roles, and even fewer hold senior-level international roles. Although it may be challenging to identify female role models, it is nevertheless important, because these role models can ease your doubts about accepting a senior role and possible serve as an inspiration. They are living proof that women can meet the challenges involved in such a role. In a broader sense, whether your role model is male or female, they can provide much-needed support in difficult times and smooth your path to a successful expatriate role. WiSER Julie Anne experienced this during her first international assignment in Peru. "They happened to have had the only female general manager in Latin America [who] was running the Peru operation," she recalled and noted that the woman's success in this role significantly increased her own chances of securing a leadership position. In the absence of role models within your organization, we recommend that you seek a role model through a professional network, or on the Board of (non-profit) organizations in which you have an interest.

Transitional Barriers

Transitional barriers demonstrate if women believe they are prepared for a transition into a next level role. It identifies how women will deal with change, challenges, uncertainty, and stress during critical points when they may move up or out of an organization. Top transitional barriers include (1) lack of a robust network; (2) lack of resilience from negative feedback.

Women continue to indicate they lack the robust networks critical for career progression. Support networks, formal or informal, are foundational to a successful professional life. An optimal method to enhance organizational influence, control of life, manage change and adapt more quickly to organizational change. They also help reduce stress and increase work satisfaction. Having mentors and sponsors in your network helps to navigate organizational politics and can be a powerful boost to career advancement. Your network determines, in part, the size of your paycheck.

When transitioning into a new role, change is a given and resilience is a must. Where there is change, there is an increased chance of both opportunities and mistakes. As 99 percent of successes derive from failures, it is counterproductive to view mistakes as a negative thing (Schoemaker 2011). Embracing change is admirable and among the respondents, there is a strong affinity for change. In fact, 78 percent responded that they thrive on change. Yet, 46 percent find it difficult to bounce back quickly when they receive negative feedback, and 57 percent find it challenging to appear confident unless they are 100 percent prepared. Therefore, it is important for women to fight the tendency to focus all of the attention on the risk associated with a new role, initiative, venture, or investment. With mistakes come key learnings, more experience, and growth.

International Barriers

When seeking international roles, there are additional barriers women may encounter. Organizations continue to overlook women for expatriate roles for a variety of reasons including a false assumption that there will be a lack of acceptance and lack of safety in the host country.

A misconception working against women is the belief that women won't be accepted in the host country. This bias has little basis in fact. The truth is, even women assigned to traditionally patriarchal regions have managed to succeed. "What I will say is I am currently working in the Middle East, and I have never worked out here before," WiSER Annette observed. "I was a little bit concerned about it, and I have to say it's the most refreshing place to work." She indicated that people with whom she worked were pleasant and cooperative. In the face of longstanding, and mostly negative, perceptions of the Middle East, she found that many men in the region were surprisingly receptive to female expatriates. Overall, gender does not have a significant bearing on how expatriates perform in their jobs, and the idea that host-country males will not accept women is patently false. Interestingly, many WiSER indicated that nationality was more frequently an issue of contention than gender was. "I don't think that being a woman was a disadvantage," said WiSER Elsa I., who worked in Latin America. "I think in fairness, [the] bigger disadvantage was the American thing."

Based on research by Adler, one of the first researchers in the field of expatriate women, "women more often experience greater difficulty commanding respect from their home country peers than from colleagues abroad, even where the cultural differences between home and host country were large" (Shortland and Altman 2011). While a host culture may regard women as naturally subordinate, local males do not necessarily put foreign women in the same category as local women. First of all, they see the expatriate woman as a senior-level professional who is deserving of respect. Secondly, they see her as a representative of her culture and/or nation. It is only then that they regard her as a woman. In many cases, they simply don't know how to classify a foreign woman who holds a position of authority. "Women expats weren't put in the same category as their own wives, their daughters, or sisters or whatever," said WiSER Anne, who lived and worked in Somalia. "We were kind of [in] a separate category." This perception was shared by WiSER Alexis, who lived and worked in Central Europe. "I am a great novelty in Prague because I'm the CEO, I'm a woman, and I'm an Australian—and maybe because I'm a foreigner they let me get away with more than they would if I was a local," she said. The unique position that female expatriates enjoy in a host country can even work to their advantage, as WiSER Carrie discovered during an assignment in South Korea. "There are so few Korean women holding those ... roles ... that they didn't really know what to expect," she said.

> If I had been a Korean man, there [would have been] tons of rules, societal rules that they would know they have to follow ... But because I was a foreigner, and because I was a woman, I just told them, "Well, the good thing is that there are no rules, and we'll just make them up as we go."

This does not suggest that women working abroad are unlikely to encounter difficulties and restrictions, however. Any expatriate, male or female, should be aware of safety issues. There are definitely certain nations that are rated as top locations for female expatriates because there are fewer safety and security issues. Different cultural codes may require women to modify their behavior, or to find different ways of collaborating. For instance, WiSER Hanan was invited to lunch by her manager in Dubai and was surprised when she entered the staff canteen. "For me, it was the first time that I saw a canteen where there was a females only area," she recalled. "So, we sat in the area that was just for females and, then, there was an area for mixed or for men, but mainly the females sat alone." Hanan realized that impromptu meetings over a cup of coffee with her manager would be difficult, and that she had to find other ways to interact with him. The key to success is to try and prevent situations that are likely to make your gender an issue. The WiSER have demonstrated that women are equally qualified in various roles across the world.

How to Break Through the Glass Ceiling and/or the Glass Border

The basic prerequisite to be considered for any professional opportunity is a combination of having the right skills, working hard and performing very well. "I've always taken my job seriously and … to the best of my ability," WiSER Stacy noted. "I do think that more opportunities will open up … if you show that you can execute and deliver on the job that you have." WiSER Erica had a similar experience. "By the time I was transferred on my first international assignment, I was managing a business with 12 countries reporting in," she said.

> I knew the products. I understood the company, and I think they felt that it would be good for me to go to a bigger market with a different culture and a very different healthcare system. They were right. I learned a lot, became a better and stronger leader … it was a good experience.

Likewise, WiSER Maria was selected for an expanded role because of her performance in the job she held. "I was recognized as a good performer. Given that I was in a global role, most of the people from the six geographic zones that we have knew about me," she recalled. "They had had two or three different persons in the role without success, and when they heard I was available, they immediately jumped on it, because I had the perfect background."

WiSER Argentina shared that she grew up in a highly disciplined environment, which she came to appreciate as she set out to develop her career. "My mother came from a tribal group called the Shangaana, in the south of Mozambique," she explained. "The men are warriors, and the women are really the ones who take care of the homes … So, it is a very hard-working group of people, and that's where I came from." Despite the hard work, however, these people maintained a positive attitude. "People laugh loud. They speak … they enjoy, and they share and meddle in each other's [lives], but pure hard work is the key that drives everything." WiSER Argentina attributes her rise to senior-level positions to this ingrained work ethic and the discipline of those early days which allowed her to face the challenges of future (professional) life.

Assuming that you have nailed the prerequisite level of high performance, the WiSER offered some professional advice to overcome barriers in order to secure either a leadership or an international role.

Make Your Intentions and Successes Known

The inability of many women to break through the glass ceiling, or the glass border, has much to do with a perennial reluctance to speak up and inform others of their career aspirations and successes. "I think that we don't necessarily do a good enough job of just saying. "If an international assignment is what you think you want ... go for it, explore it ... The worst thing that anyone can say is, 'no'," said WiSER Meredith. It is not in your interest to sit back and wait until you are noticed. You may be waiting a long, long time—or worse yet, you may never find yourself on the short list for an international opportunity.

It is best to be explicit about your goals, and to clarify what you need in order to be successful. "I think many people do not get where they want to be because they do not 'speak up,'" said WiSER Argentina. "They are too afraid to try. They do not want to take the risk of a 'no.'" In taking a more assertive attitude at her organization, WiSER Nina said she followed the example of her male colleagues. "I realized that men are much better in saying what they want than women," she observed. "I also realized that you have to say what you want, and not assume others know." She recalled that, when she learned about an exptriate assignment in London, she expressed an interest in the job. "I said that very early on, and everybody said, 'Oh, you are too young,'" she recalled. They pointed to her lack of experience and her lack of familiarity with the organization as a whole. "I said, 'Well, so what—I will learn,'" she said. "I said it several times, and then, I wrote a letter to our secretary general, and I said next time the job is available, I am interested." Eventually, she did get the coveted position in London.

The difference in gender communication styles is highlighted by a humorous anecdote that WiSER Tuulia shared. She recalled that she was talking to some friends about mountain climbing, and she asked them if they had reached a particular peak that was considered rather daunting. WiSER Tuulia noted that one woman, who had climbed that peak on two expeditions, only briefly mentioned this fact. At the same time, her male friend, who had climbed the peak just once, described the adventure in great detail and emphasized the risks involved. Finally, another person involved in the conversation began to laugh and said, "Did you notice the lady has been there twice, and the guy is just screaming about it?" The moral of the story is, if you want to be heard, you may need to flex your communication style to ensure that your message is heard.

Although you may be committed to speaking up for yourself, it often proves challenging to own success and demand recognition—and cultural norms sometimes get in the way. In some Eastern cultures, the view that a woman should be seen and not heard remains quite prevalent. As WiSER Alicia indicated, however, speaking up is a challenge that we can meet. "Growing up, I was very quiet, very reserved, so very, very shy," she told us. "I was a middle child; I wouldn't even speak to an adult, wouldn't do any public speaking, nothing. And to this day, I am much more reserved." In her professional life, however, she encountered strong managers who insisted she learn to express her views. "I would never speak up in meetings," she recalled. "I would go to them after the meeting, and I had one manager tell me, 'I'm not going to listen to you unless you have enough guts to say it in the meeting.'" While such experiences were uncomfortable, they pushed her to develop her ability to make herself heard, to the benefit of her career.

Leverage the Career Planning Process

It's never too early to begin setting professional goals and managing your career. Creating a career plan may seem daunting, but you can demystify the process with the help of an effective coach. Once you have created your career plan, leverage it to create visibility for your successes, and to promote the ways in which your work supports the organization in its efforts to achieve its goals. WiSER Lindsay emphasized the need to develop a career plan, and she revealed that, when she took her first HR director role, her boss insisted that she develop one. "What's a career plan?" she recalled thinking. "I found it really hard, and I clearly remember to this day going into my new management director's office and saying, 'Steve, I really need your help because I don't really know what I'm doing here.'" At that point her manager helped her plot out the plan on a whiteboard. The exercise helped her to consider her career aspirations. She started with a goal and reverse-engineered the path needed to get there. With her manager's help, she considered sectors, countries, roles, and experiences that she required, such as acquisition experience. "It's amazing," she said. "I could take that 'career plan' out of the cover and show it to you, and you could see I have ticked off everything that I said I would do." She added, "No, I haven't done it in the right order, but pretty much everything that I said I'd do, I've done during that time."

As noted, career management can also serve as a vehicle to increase your organizational visibility and promote your wins. "Something I absolutely insist on is that I always make sure I have goals every single year," said WiSER Laura. She added that these goals and performance objectives were always aligned to the organization and the manager she was supporting. Furthermore, she insisted that these goals and objectives were reviewed at least twice a year. Although she realizes that this approach is not "rocket science," she found it to work exceedingly well. "If my manager or whoever at that time wasn't willing to take the time to do that with me, I would do it," she said. "And I would religiously go through and say, 'Okay, this is what I've accomplished this year, this is what went well, and this is what didn't go well." She would then focus on two or three areas of potential improvement and develop a strategy to accomplish this. She indicated that this process went further when she sat with supervisors—and even managers above her supervisor—to carefully review goals, risks, and accomplishments. "Even though some of the time I am sure these people would roll their eyes and say, 'Oh, it's her again' … I make sure that they know I have a vision," she added. "I have a plan, and this is where I want to be."

It is important to realize that career planning is not just about securing promotions and climbing the career ladder. When setting professional goals, other factors, such as personal satisfaction, personal sensibilities, and personal values, should be taken into consideration. Once you have decided that you want to pursue a leadership or international role, follow your goals and don't give up. Know what you want, communicate it, and pursue it.

Take Creative Paths to Lasso a Leadership or Expatriate Role

Imagine stepping stones in a pond that lead to the other side. Some may prefer to cross by using the biggest, most visible, stones. Others may explore those stones that sit slightly below the surface, zigzagging across the pond, but still manage to get to the other side. Meanwhile, some might be halfway across the pond when they realize that they need to backtrack and take a different path in order to get to the other side. If getting to the other side is your goal, there is no wrong way to get there. Keep your eyes on the prize.

Consider volunteering for an especially challenging assignment, perhaps a project or joining work streams, that needs someone to spearhead success. Strong performance and the willingness to step up when others are not will give you visibility, and could result in a fantastic opportunity. Even when results aren't ideal, skills can still be learned. WiSER Kelli indicated that volunteering for certain tasks enabled her to gain experience that made her a viable candidate for promotion down the road. "It really wasn't even my responsibility and my role, but I stepped [in] and said … 'I can work on that project,'" she said. "Then, when you've gotten some experience, of course, you are the one that they turn to then in the future."

Some options to get an expatriate role may include accepting a short-term international project in order to demonstrate your global agility. WiSER Tuulia revealed that she was originally offered a four-month assignment to use her expertise from the Finland office and apply it to the development of similar standards and processes in the German office. She accepted the four-month assignment and several years later still remained in Germany. Although it didn't start as an expatriate assignment, her successes over a brief period of time expanded the opportunity. Some WiSER have gone so far as to accept a position below their current level to gain international experience. "I did very well for myself in my various jobs," recalled WiSER Janice. "I lived in Atlanta, and then, I decided I needed more international experience on my resume, because I didn't really have any. Even though my clients were big firms, I never had big international clients." Ultimately, WiSER Janice agreed to accept a position as a director even though she had already secured vice president status. Although the job was a step down in terms of position and proved to be a lateral move in terms of salary, it opened the door to an exciting overseas assignment in London within two years.

The important message the WiSER conveyed, is to be open to creative career pathing, especially when looking to work abroad. Otherwise, you severely limit your options. WiSER Andrea indicated that people who are too specific in their goals often get frustrated when they don't secure the position they want. "So, I always try to keep it very flexible," she added. By considering a wider variety of appropriate options, she found that she was more likely to find a position that was satisfying.

Look Before You Leap

Even if working abroad has not been your lifelong plan, it can be for you. Despite their success in international roles, some of the WiSER revealed that they did have doubts about their decision to accept an expatriate assignment. However, "This doesn't mean that you should give into those doubts," WiSER Kelli said. Before accepting an international role, it is important to (1) identify a role that is a good fit, (2) determine if the expatriate role is with a female friendly employer or environment, (3) consider implications of expatriating solo, with a trailing spouse, and/or other family members. First, it is important to identify a geography and organizational climate that is a fit for you. It is essential to do your homework in order to truly understand the market and other relevant variables, including safety, living conditions, schools, proximity to daily activities, and so forth. Think it through from all angles, such as professional implications, family considerations, and personal motivations. Thoroughly researching a potential assignment will prepare you to manage the challenges. Download the Women Leaders Toolkit from the BEP Publishing website for additional tools and resources.

WiSER Elsa L. cautions people considering an international assignment to think deeply about the implications of moving to a wholly new environment. "If you are coming from a small … community, and you suddenly find yourself in Sao Paolo, with 16 million people, you have to think about the fact that you are going [somewhere] … very different from what you've known," she said. WiSER Diane, who worked for various NGOs in Asia added:

You are going to work in countries—maybe—that are in conflict, or you are going to be working in places where there is extreme poverty. So, the sort of person who is attracted to that, by personality, is unlikely to be someone who wants a clean break from the suburbs, or catches the same bus to work every day, and has gone through a very clear pathway after [she] finished school.

Second, if you are considering an employer who provides international opportunities, it is also important to determine whether they are female friendly. WiSER Nathalie K. noted that she works for just such an organization. "I've been very lucky in that sense, that throughout my career, I've had great line managers who always wanted to see me grow and develop—always open to listen, always looking for new opportunities," she said. "So, the moment I said, 'Can I go to Spain?' they listened." She added that her managers not only offered encouragement, but also asked searching questions that led her to think deeply about her decisions. In her female-friendly firm, she encountered a corporate culture where managers encouraged employees to identify their goals and then helped them to achieve these goals. There are various hubs such as Fairygodboss and Inhersight that effectively aggregate information on how strong an employer is when it comes to being female friendly.

Third, WiSER Joanne stressed the importance of thinking through every aspect of a potential move. The emerging trend in expatriation highlights that more single women are taking international roles. As a single woman, a potential challenge is building new relationships. WiSER Fiona recalled: "I was in a meeting with probably 12 senior women out of some 400 scientists and only two among us were in a functioning relationship and that's the toll that it takes on women."

If you have a family that will come with you, "you need to think whether or not this is a good move for your family because it does change and impact everyone in the family," WiSER Joanne said. "This isn't just about your position or your move." Without familial support, your chances of succeeding will be undermined. "If your family is absolutely against moving with you, don't" WiSER Martine said. Many expatriate women have partners and or families. Among the WiSER, 82 percent were either married or had a serious partner. Only 12 percent of the WiSER were divorced, which is lower than many national divorce rate statistics. The WiSER who had partners clearly indicated that their partner's support was seminal to their success abroad. Many went on to share stories of how their partners—many of whom had a successful career in their home country—chose to stay at home or back burner their career for their duration abroad. Among WiSER with a trailing spouse, 58 percent reported that their partner worked in the host country (most often found on their own), and 42 percent said that their partner either put his career on hold to take care of the family in the host country or did not find work.

It is dawning on many international organizations that facilitating dual-career options will increase their international talent pool and contribute to the willingness of their employees to consider career options requiring international mobility. Sudden changes in professional life such as the transition to stop working and become a full-time husband, or even stay-at-home father are difficult at best. This is further compounded because trailing-spouse environments are still dominated by women. Considering the criticality of managing dual careers and the impact that expatriating will have on a dual-career household, it is very important to discuss the consequences with your partner when you are the "leading lady." As WiSER Joanne thoughtfully discussed, "We always made the decision on how our careers would go, which one we would follow, and whatever we choose … we have to have that constant conversation because it's very, very hard in most families for the male to take a second chair after they have been the first chair for all their lives. So, you have to just manage to have an open dialogue so that you maintain a good relationship in that conversation. Whether or not working in the host country for your trailing spouse is an option, the most important thing you can do is to ensure that behind you, there still is a "great man," who supports you."

If dual career options are not available, determine if there are different types of work that may be permitted within the host country. Sometimes it is difficult to get a work permit to work for a large organization, in the host country, but a trailing partner may be able to start a small business or do some consulting. Groups like the United Nations sponsor workers in various nations because of their global status. Furthermore, there are a growing number of opportunities to work remotely or for a virtual organization, such as online universities. Male trailing spouse, Alan, shared that he is sometimes asked why he wanted to go off to foreign parts, trailing in his wife's professional wake. His answer:

> Because it is the best darn fun you can legally have, that's why. Learning another language and culture is a big opportunity for you and the family to broaden your horizons. See how other country's people live, work and play. Your children will benefit a thousand-fold from the experience, in many ways not possible back home.

WiSER Fiona concluded that, if one wants to succeed on an international assignment, you need to "be curious and have a sense of humor." As WiSER Magi shared, "the decision about whether or not to work and live overseas should ultimately be a personal choice ... and will be fulfilling when aligned with values."

It's a Wrap!

Although women are ready and willing to take on leadership and expatriate roles, there is a false assumption that they are not interested in such roles. Barriers to women's professional advancement can be segmented into individual, organizational, transitional, and international barriers. Barriers that contribute to stalling women from moving into either leadership or international roles can be overcome by performing well, sharing both career aspirations and successes, leveraging the career planning process, and taking creative career paths to get to your goal. As per WiSER Lillian, "If expatriating is something that interests you then ... nothing should stop you from doing what you want to do."

New beginnings always present new opportunities accompanied with new challenges. Therefore, it is important to make sure the country and organization are a fit for you and for others accompanying you. The WiSER we interviewed described their international experience as a period that deeply enriched their lives. "Yes, I would do it again," said WiSER Allyson, with a touch of humor. "It's like childbirth. You put the bad out of your mind, and you only remember all the good of it." WiSER Tuulia agreed. "In retrospect, the challenges and difficulties were a simple nuisance," she said. "It wasn't the end of the world … I think people have more regrets about the things they don't do than the ones they do."

SECTION II

CHAPTER 3

WiSER Leadership Competencies

Because I am a woman, I must make unusual efforts to succeed. If I fail, no one will say, she doesn't have what it takes. They will say, women don't have what it takes.

—*Clare Boothe Luce*

Being an expat feeds my sense of adventure and my sense of always wanting to challenge myself, to see how far I can push myself.

—*Wiser Fiona*

To reach strong performance in an expatriate role, it is important to understand and master global leadership competencies. Competencies are a combination of knowledge, skills, and abilities, demonstrated through observable and measurable behavior. Global leadership competencies are commonly categorized as leading the organization, leading self and leading others, and will elevate global leadership capabilities.

Future leaders can better prepare for global roles by understanding who they are, how they work with others, and how other cultures prefer to work with them. By understanding key competencies for success in an international role, men and women can achieve the same high level of performance in a new country.

When considering global leadership competency models, bear in mind that they have been developed with a sample set consisting primarily of men, who are the majority of expatriates. Global leadership competencies differ from general leadership competencies because of the added complexity of different countries and cultures involved. Despite the fact that expatriate assignments typically range between three to five times the cost of a comparable local employee, there is often a lack of clarity regarding the competencies for success. Fortunately, global leadership competencies can be coached and developed. As leaders in international roles cultivate competencies for success, it is important to note that it is equally important to remain an authentic leader. As WiSER Ayesha explained: "I am a woman. I am a professional. I am myself. ... Just be yourself, and you know what, half the battle is won." Developing global leadership competencies is the remaining half of the battle!

Harvard Business Review published prevalent global leadership competencies, divided into five dominant themes, that are valid both for men and women (Giles 2016).

Demonstrates Strong Ethics and Provides a Sense of Safety

This theme is all about creating a safe and trusting environment by leading with high ethical standards, commitment to fairness, and trustworthiness by following through and clearly communicating expectations.

Empowers Others to Self-Organize

This theme describes how effective leaders provide clear direction, and enable individuals to take action, control their work, and make decisions autonomously. They trust and support individuals to work independently.

Shows Openness to New Ideas and Fosters Organizational Learning

This theme notes that strong leaders are flexible to new ideas and opinions, and foster life-long learning.

Nurtures Growth

This theme focuses on leaders committing to training, coaching, and developing the next-generation of leaders.

Fosters a Sense of Connection and Belonging

This theme highlights our human need to have interpersonal connections and a strong sense of team.

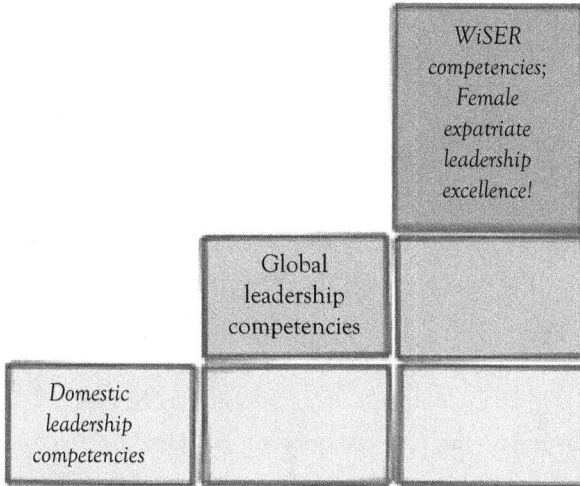

Figure 3.1 Building blocks to female expatriate leadership excellence

These global leadership competencies are important for both men and women to develop and master in order to be successful in a global role. However, they will only get women in expatriate roles so far, because female expatriate leaders are in a unique position compared to both the female domestic leader and the male expatriate leader (Figure 3.1).

Our groundbreaking research has uncovered that there are four additional competencies that are shared among WiSER!

- **Self-awareness**: Knowing your strengths and weaknesses, likes and dislikes—which are all based on your values—and using this knowledge to make critical decisions
- **Conscious Imbalance**: Tipping the scales toward what gives you energy and fulfillment with the realization that the scales will need to be rebalanced on a regular basis
- **Active Career Management**: Knowing what you want from your career and working with intention to achieve those goals
- **Operating Outside Your Comfort Zone**: Embracing challenges coming from new experiences by tolerating ambiguity and remaining calm

We will take you on in-depth exploration of these competencies in Chapters 4 through 7.

Why Female Expatriate Leaders Are in a Unique Position

Among the women we interviewed, we discerned tremendous differences, and found some striking similarities. The data we consolidated demonstrates that there is a correlation among WiSER as a sample group, therefore the WiSER are spread across a single bell curve relative to each competency. The bell curve for WiSER competencies is different than the bell curve for domestic female leaders or the bell curve for expatriate male leaders (Figure 3.2). Let us illustrate our point by asking you a simple question. "Do you work hard?" Your answer may be "yes" or "no"—it is not all that important. The real question is, "How do you know?" You probably know because you have compared yourself to other people: colleagues, friends, and acquaintances. However, each culture has its own criteria for what constitutes "hard work." In Germany, for instance working 50 hours a week is considered working hard; whereas in Japan the standards increase considerably and working 80 hours a week is considered to be working hard. In fact, there is even a Japanese term, "karoshi," that roughly translates to "work yourself to death."

The workers in Germany are scattered across a single bell curve whereas the Japanese are scattered across a separate, parallel bell curve. Although both bell curves plot the answer to the "do you work hard?" question, it would be inaccurate to plot them all on a single bell curve. In the same way, when comparing WiSER competencies, we have essentially separate, parallel bell curves, or norms when comparing expatriate women to expatriate men and domestic women (Figure 3.3).

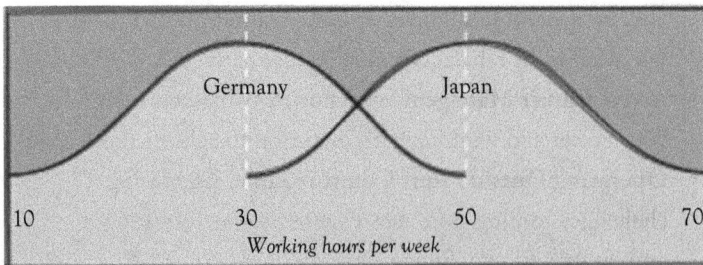

Figure 3.2 Bell curve average working hours per week for Germany and Japan

Note: the hours used are not based on statistical data.

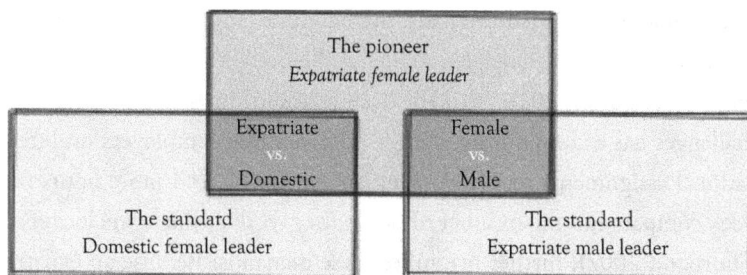

Figure 3.3 The expatriate female leader

A good example of accomplishing the same feat while facing different challenges is that of the first person to reach the summit of Mount Everest. Many mistakenly credit only Sir Edmund Hillary for this accomplishment. The first ascent was actually completed in 1953 by both Edmund Hillary and Tenzing Norgay. Edmund Hillary is commonly recognized whereas Tenzing Norgay is obscure. He was the Sherpa who accompanied Hillary. Sherpas have been recognized for their strength and climbing capabilities since the time European mountaineers first arrived and employed their services as guides and porters. Norgay carried the climbing supplies, served as the navigator, set up camps, and had the natural ability of the Sherpa people. Hillary was unfamiliar with this terrain, had formally prepared by climbing various mountains in different countries around the world, and had to rely on the guidance of another. We can assume that either of these men would describe their climb to the top as extremely difficult and rewarding.

Expatriate Female Leader versus Domestic Female Leader

While women in leadership positions encounter barriers in their home country, this is further compounded because they also have to overcome barriers in their host countries (Tung 2005). Additionally, frequently cited challenges for working women include the double "burden syndrome" and the "anytime, anywhere" performance model. The "double burden" syndrome, means that women are responsible for work and the majority of the household responsibilities. A recent study found that, with some variations per nation, working women do almost 40 percent more household chores than men with some variability by nation

(Independent 2017). Additionally, the "anytime, anywhere" performance model calls for top managers to make themselves available with great agility (McKinsey 2010, 6). The interrelationship between these two challenges has a compounding effect. The fact that "employees on international assignments report working an average of 13.4 more hours per week compared to the number of hours they work at the home location" (Shortland 2007), further magnifies these demands. Because an expatriate environment exacerbates domestic challenges 10-fold, global female leaders face unique challenges.

Expatriate Female Leader versus Expatriate Male Leader

Do male expatriate counterparts not possess or need to demonstrate WiSER competencies? In German the answer would be "jein" (a combination of yes and no). Yes, male expatriates do need to actively manage their career and they do need to be self-aware. They will face balancing and rebalancing their priorities and they also will need to be able to operate outside of their comfort zone. However, for men the circumstances and challenges are simply different than for women. Female expatriates are still pioneering in these roles whereas male expatriates are the "standard."

A level playing field is a situation in which everyone has the same chance of succeeding. In business, both men and women have to play the game by the same rules, in the same field, with the same referees so to speak. When the "game" of business was created by men, for men, with male referees, it is disadvantageous to women who want to play. Sociologists refer to this as "male advantaging," we call it an "un-level" playing field.

The powerful effects of implicit bias and lack of trust and psychological safety are leading factors contributing to this bell curve. In expatriate roles, these factors are further exaggerated.

Implicit Bias

Research continues to demonstrate that gender diversity leads to better organizational performance: it makes us more creative, diligent, and hard-working. However, biases, whether they be conscious or implicit, increase challenges that women expatriates face once in an international role, especially an international leadership role.

First, traditional societal expectations, which vary across nations and cultures, enhance the challenges expatriate women face. Although progress has been made, the traditional view regarding a man's and a woman's role in the family and at work remains deeply entrenched: men work, and women take care of the home and the children.

Both women and men have a range of career choices, which may include working full-time or part-time, consulting, or staying at home. Nevertheless, we do not see an abundance of either female executives or stay-at-home dads. In most cultures, it is generally accepted that women with children can work. However, people don't know how to react when a woman is the primary breadwinner of a family, while her husband is the stay-at-home dad. Luckily, WiSER are changing societal expectations, one step at a time. WiSER Alicia described the ways in which such social and cultural expectations affected the dynamic of her and her husband's roles within her own family. "My husband ... was expected to be the breadwinner of the family," she said. "[For the] wife, it was okay to have a job, but not a high career job. So, it was a lot of social pressure to be just the opposite of that situation and we also had to shift our families' social, cultural expectations." WiSER Sezin shared with us the traditional expectations concerning women in her country. "I'm from the modern Turkey," she said. "But still, traditionally, we do expect ... women to do so much more in a household ... My mom was always angry with me that I wouldn't be cooking for my daughter the type of food that she would be cooking for me ... and that I would prefer to have somebody else make it for her." Societal expectations get even trickier when expatriating. In addition to meeting domestic societal expectations, expatriate female leaders face societal expectations of the host country and the expatriate community.

Second, implicit biases held by others can require women to prove themselves more than men. "It's always different when you are a woman," WiSER Esther said. "The challenge for you as a leader ... is to demonstrate that it does not make a big difference." She added, "It's not that you are going to behave like a man. I have never behaved like a male leader, but at the same time, the challenge was to show that women are just as efficient as men in carrying out their task."

Third, when teams are comprised of both men and women, others may believe they are less effective because they often have what appears to be non-productive conflicts and a lengthier storming, norming, to performing cycle. In reality, conflict is not necessarily a sign that things are going wrong or that they can't be resolved. Rather, the team is working through broadly differing information, perspectives, and worldviews that in the end results in innovation, better problem solving, and accurate decision-making (Phillips 2016). Diverse teams should celebrate their outcomes and make sure that those evaluating them know about the successes. Conscious or unconscious biases about gender diverse groups can undermine the very benefits of diversity.

Lack of Trust and Psychological Safety

"Psychological safety," a term introduced by Harvard Business School Professor Amy Edmondson, is "a shared belief that the team is safe for interpersonal risk taking" (Edmondson 2014). The number one trait that was shared among Google's most successful teams is psychological safety (Lebowitz 2015). In a safe environment, employees can be engaged, express themselves freely, take risks and experiment, without the fear of failure or retribution. They tend to be more relaxed, which allows for higher thinking and greater capacity for social engagement, innovation, creativity, and ambition. Research has shown that just 3 in 10 U.S. employees strongly agree that their opinions seem to count at work and feel they can express themselves without the fear of failure or retribution. Among diverse populations, this number is undoubtedly lower. However, if that ratio were to increase to 6 in 10, turnover in organizations could be reduced by 27 percent, safety incidents by 40 percent, productivity increased by 12 percent (Herway 2017).

Psychological safety is a broader notion than trust and includes caring and trusting one another and respecting each other's capabilities. Where psych safety is something that is felt within a group, trust begins one on one, in relationships. Notably, trust is significantly lower now than a generation ago, with only 49 percent of employees trusting senior management and only 28 percent believing that CEOs are a credible source of information (Covey). When trust is low, it places a hidden "tax" on every transaction: every communication, every interaction, every strategy, every decision is taxed, bringing speed down and sending costs up. Trust is foundational to change, and it is essential to dismantling barriers stopping women from moving into leadership roles. Trust cultivates diversity. It also happens to be the foundation of good leadership! For WiSER Diane, the establishment of trust is a foundational piece in building effective leadership. Now that she is a leader herself, she gives her people the same amount of trust and operating space she received early in her career:

> I had feedback from my staff … it was quite a unique experience for them working for me, because I absolutely focused on how I could really develop them into spaces that they probably never thought of going before. Many of them said to me that it was the first time that they had ever had somebody going for that amount of trust in their ability to do or to demonstrate or to perform in an area where they hadn't demonstrated success [yet].

Strong leaders understand how to build trust in relationships and psychological safety in teams to best employ the talents of people and allow them to take risks and make mistakes. As mentioned earlier, most successes derive from failures and it is counterproductive to view mistakes as a negative thing. Schoemaker goes as far as to recommend that global organizations plan and promote mistakes in order to improve learning and move on to the next level (Schoemaker 2011).

Trust + Risk-taking + Evaluation = (Tremendous) Growth

Research shows that women who make mistakes in traditionally male occupations are judged much more harshly than their male counterparts who make mistakes (Huston 2016). Regardless of occupation, "women's mistakes tend to be given more weight and remembered longer than men's" (Williams 2014). Therefore, risk taking is not as simple as it may seem for women. As one of the few—or maybe even the first—expatriate women in an executive position in the host country, her actions will be closely monitored by many people. This is not necessarily because she is a foreigner, but it is more likely because she is a female foreigner. WiSER Elsa L. noted that she was the first female head of her organization in Paraguay, and therefore, she experienced what it was like to be a successful woman in a machismo society. "[It] was like big news," she recalled. "I mean the newspapers came out ... to interview me ... because people were surprised." She added that, to some extent, she became a victim of her own celebrity. "There was nowhere that I could go that I was not—I mean even the supermarket—that I was not the director general of the [organization]." She stressed that there was a real need for caution and prudence, given that people were observing her every move. "You have to be a little careful of what you say and the opinions you give, because then you find yourself being quoted, sometimes misquoted," she said. The good news is, having such a high visibility also puts you in a position where you can be very influential and achieve many great things.

As we said, you are likely to stand out—not only in the host country, but also in your organization. You are an example: a role model for other women within the organization, in the country, and perhaps even in the world. If you make a mistake—or worse yet, if you fail—the consequences of your misstep will move beyond the organizational effect. When she was in Peru, WiSER Julie Anne had a female colleague who left the country after having been there for only three days. "It was the worst thing ever," she remembered, "It's such an insult to the country ... If you are lucky enough to get one of these assignments, you better stick it out, because you ruin it for other women if you're not able to stick it out." Although there is great pressure involved in being a role model, not many of us have such an opportunity.

Women tend to dwell on all the things they can't do well, but hardly take time to think about all their strengths. The key to success lies in leveraging your strengths to confidently take calculated risks. Learn to view a mistake as a learning experience that leads to growth. Overcome the tendency to focus all of your attention on the risk associated with a new initiative, venture, or investment. Rather, balance your view of risk with excitement about the potential reward. Not only should you allow yourself to make mistakes, but you should also forgive yourself in advance. You are in an intense and entirely new situation. As WiSER Martha told us: "... I think [you should] just go for it and be willing to make mistakes and to acknowledge those mistakes." The key to dealing with mistakes is to manage them. Inform the appropriate parties when a mistake is likely to affect them, take steps to remedy the error, ask for assistance to "fix it," and finally, learn from your mistakes. They will undoubtedly lead to good things.

Business success is correlated with risk-taking. Therefore, it is important for women to fight the tendency to focus all of the attention on the risk associated with a new role, initiative, venture, or investment. At the same time, it is important for organizations to foster an environment of both trust and psychological safety where leaders encourage employees to take risks and learn from mistakes. With mistakes come key learnings, more experience, and growth.

Developing Competencies

Many global leadership skills can be acquired or enhanced with relative ease. Competencies, however, are much more difficult to master, because they are a combination of knowledge, skills, and abilities which are exhibited in behavior patterns. After coaching hundreds of professionals over many years in many countries, we know that entrenched behavior is difficult to change yet doable (Figure 3.4). Neuroscience research continues to show that the human brain is highly pliable. The brain is always forming new connections, forming and reforming them, allowing new behaviors to be learned. "This process of neuroplasticity happens thousands of times a day, giving us enormous potential to change if we put awareness, effort

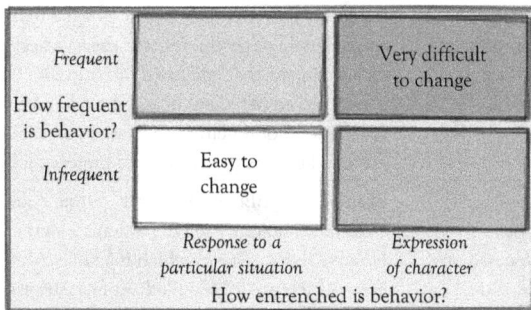

Figure 3.4 Changeability of behavior

Source: HBR essentials: coaching and mentoring. Adapted from James Waldrop.

and commitment into making it happen" (Langley 2012). Download the Women Leaders Toolkit from the BEP Publishing website for additional tools and resources.

Self-discovery is a good starting point to develop competencies. We recommend women assess themselves against a standard set of global leadership competencies, and the WiSER competencies. Next, focus on enhancing a modest number of competencies that will be most beneficial to your expatriate assignment. There are four progressive stages to mastering competencies which will lead to success. Some competencies will be easier to develop than others because of where your own personal strengths lie. In the following chart, examples are provided to help visualize the different levels of competency development ranging from Phase 1 (lowest level of mastery) to Phase 4 (highest level of mastery) (Table 3.1, Adams 2018).

Table 3.1 Phases to develop competencies. Adapted from conscious competence model, Gordon Training International

Phase 4 Unaware—competent You do the right thing without even having to think about it	Example—WiSER Gabriel: "The Board decided to send me to Mexico to be the CEO and build up their business for Mexico and Central America. I needed to build up big revenue in the first year. You have a completely different situation, you have a different culture, you have different people, you have different goals. I was used to change, adapting very fast, and bringing results. I was two years in Mexico, and we already had 30 million in turnover in the first year."
Phase 3 Aware—competent You are very focused on doing the right thing and you are succeeding	Example—WiSER Hanan relocated from Australia to Dubai. After six or seven months, she started wearing the local clothing called Abaya. She did that because it seemed more respectful because she was working for a local company that employed many locals. This simple action helped her blend in and she felt more comfortable b/c she was not soliciting unwanted stares. Her co-workers found it to be thoughtful and professional.
Phase 2 Aware—incompetent You are very focused on doing the right thing but still make mistakes	Example—WiSER Abby relocated from America to Singapore and is invited to participate in the annual Holiday "Lucky Draw," which is a raffle. Abby won the draw, which was a $400 iPod. At first, she was excited then quickly felt guilty b/c she was a firm partner and felt that it would have been better if someone else won.

	However, she didn't want to offend anyone, so she kept the gift. One week later, somebody told her that partners are supposed to give the gifts back. Oh, if only somebody had told Abby ahead of time.
Phase 1 Unaware— incompetent You make mistakes, but you are not aware that you do	Example—For your international assignment, you relocate to Malaysia, which is heavily Islamic. For the annual holiday gift, without further consideration, you present your staff with a basket filled with fruit, pork sausage, and wine.

It's a Wrap!

Working and living abroad presents its unique opportunities and challenges, for women in particular. Theoretically, women expats leaders sit on a different bell curve than male expats or domestic female leaders. Factors contributing to this separate bell curve include the "double burden" syndrom, the "anywhere anytime" performance model, and an unlevel playing field. Implicit bias, and lack of trust and psychological safety are key reasons why the playing field is unlevel. Mastering competencies, which are a combination of knowledge, skills and abilities, can be challenging, yet is most definitely doable. Practicing global leadership competencies and WiSER competencies will lead to a smoother transition to an expatriate role and reduce ramp up time to high performance. The foundational information and research in this chapter demonstrates that mastering four WiSER competencies will position women to be successful leaders in senior-level expatriate roles.

CHAPTER 4

Self-Awareness

As you become clearer about who you really are, you'll be better able to decide what is best for you—the first time around.

—Oprah Winfrey

I remember how naive I was and yet how clearly I saw my future that last year of high school. I see my [younger] self with dangling legs, sitting on a school bench and saying, I don't know what I want to be, but I want to do something that has to do with international culture and administration—which is exactly what I ended up doing.

—WiSER Britta

"Mirror, mirror on the wall, who's the fairest of them all?" Ah-h-h, this is a classic example of self-awareness—or is it? How self-aware are you? Sometimes, our sense of who we are isn't necessarily shared by those around us. Do you see yourself as others see you? What does it mean to be self-aware? For the purposes of our study, we defined the competency "Self-awareness" as follows:

Self-awareness
Knowing your strengths and weaknesses, likes and dislikes—which are all based on your values—and using this knowledge to make critical decisions.
<ul><li>You have a strong understanding of your values, personal strengths, weaknesses, opportunities, and limits.</li><li>You know in which situations you will thrive and in which you will feel stressed.</li><li>You trust yourself and follow your intuition.</li><li>You know how you differ from others and accept these differences.</li><li>You know how you are perceived by others.</li><li>You spend your time on what is important and quickly zero in on the critical few and put the trivial many aside.</li><li>You demonstrate the ability to strengthen your own weaknesses through training and development.</li></ul>

82 percent of the WiSER demonstrated self-awareness. Our research has shown that the presence of self-awareness was highest among women working in not-for-profit organizations (100 percent), followed by women working in governmental organizations (88 percent), and women in for-profit organizations (83 percent). Also, those women who had self-initiated their expatriation showed more self-awareness than women who were sent abroad by their organization, at 94 percent and 77 percent, respectively. This could be explained by the fact that, when you self-initiate your move abroad, you have already considered all the decisions that must be made regarding the country, the new job, and various aspects involving the move. Therefore, you are more fully aware, in general. In our research, we found that those WiSER who demonstrated a high degree of self-awareness took their careers into their own hands through active career management more often than the WiSER who did not show a high level of self-awareness, at 69 percent and 55 percent, respectively. All of this points to the fact that you are better able to steer your career when you know what you want—and also, what you don't want.

On the spectrum of self-awareness, where do you think you fall? Where would you like to be? What steps can you take to get there?

Unaware of who I am ◄——— **I KNOW WHO I AM** ———► I know best

Self-awareness, or learning about yourself, is important to build a successful career. Values serve as the basis for self-awareness. Some of the most significant outcomes of self-awareness are heightened emotional intelligence and improved decision making. Greater emotional intelligence will position you to anticipate your emotional reaction to various people and situations, and to flex as needed in order to achieve an effective outcome. Self-awareness also serves as a compass to drive effective decision making. Finally, being aware of your strengths and weaknesses, likes and dislikes, enables you to increase engagement and energy.

In an international role, the complexities involved demand an even greater sense of self-awareness. It will help you decide whether to adapt or not to adapt in your new environment. Do you know how you differ from others, and do you accept these differences? Do you know the effect of these differences when you operate in a different cultural environment?

Like the queen in the fairy tale "Snow White," you could use a "mirror"—that is, an assessment tool—to see what you look like. Assessment tools can help you gain insights into your values, qualities, talents, and interests. Tools like DiSC, Hogan (HDS), MBTI, and Gallup Strengths Finder are all excellent starting points. To go a step further, there are tools that will provide 360° input from subordinates, peers, and managers, so you can better understand how others assess your capabilities. Self-awareness, after all, is not just how we see ourselves; it also considers the way others see us. As WiSER Heidi aptly said: "I think making any move—whether it's from one institution to another or one country to another—makes you reassess how you look at yourself, and how other people look at you." Cultural differences may influence how you are perceived in a domestic versus international setting and self-awareness will help you manage others' perception of you. Reassessing yourself is especially important when you are in a country with different cultural values than your own. As L. Robert Kohls, an expert in the field of internationalism, noted, "By lowering our defenses and viewing ourselves through the eyes of people from other cultures—from what is called the cross-cultural perspective—we can get a strikingly fresh view of ourselves" (Kohls 2001). Revealed and concealed culture impacts how people from a different culture perceive you. For example, Americans value confident opinions and questions when collaborating, whereas that same behavior is seen as brash in China. This one example alone demonstrates that the "mirror" is indeed a magic mirror: depending on where you are, you will look different.

Just like the queen in "Snow White," the image the mirror reveals may be unsettling and may lead you to make changes. Similarly, after identifying your strengths and development areas based on assessments (the mirror) and 360° feedback, targeted changes may be made. "I did 360 [-degree] feedback frequently," revealed WiSER Laura. "Some people hate that, but I love it, because [I] learn so much about myself and others and interactions, like how to deal with people. I think that's one of my key success factors."

When making those changes, make sure that they are noticed by the right people in order to influence their perception of the changes you are making. "When I got promoted, that was kind of a big milestone," said

WiSER Allyson. "It was also [a] really good learning experience, because … I got some really good advice when I was promoted." Among the most valuable pieces of advice she received was to be attentive to other people's perceptions of her. "There was some concern about my level of conduct," she recalled.

> I didn't think I was doing the things that people said I was doing, because that wasn't my impression of how I was behaving—and I got a really good piece of advice during that time that said it doesn't matter what you think you're acting like. What matters is what other people think that you're acting like.

She recognized that the impressions of others played a crucial role in her effectiveness. "You have to kind of look at it from other people's perspective," she added. "It helped me to just take a step back and look at myself, … not only so it can help me progress, but also just as a person." Self-assessment is valuable at any career juncture.

Identifying Your Values

The first step leading to self-awareness is to identify your values, which are the essence of who you are as a person. Whether or not you are consciously aware of your values, every individual has a core set of personal values. Values can range from practical, such as the belief in hard work and punctuality, to the more abstract, like a belief in self-reliance, concern for others, and harmony of purpose. When we examine the lives of others, we often see how personal values guided them, and in some cases even inspired others to rise to the top of their capabilities. Individuals that may come to mind include notable figures like Nelson Mandela, Mahatma Gandhi, or Mother Teresa.

Values differ from person to person, and household to household, and many of them are shaped in our formative years. The WiSER shared childhood memories that had a profound impact on the rest of their lives. WiSER Julie's parents were immigrants to Canada and her life was filled with moving around for her father's job, a working mother and memories of growing up on a blueberry farm. She shared that the main principles in her childhood home were "respect for one another, love for one another, looking out for each other, respecting our elders." In a similar vein, WiSER Kelli told us that her parents' expatriate backgrounds helped to shape her values and interests. "My parents lived—and my father worked—in … Ethiopia …or about four years, just before I was born," she revealed. "They had that kind of expatriate background and, of course, they always told great stories about that when we were kids." She indicated these stories fueled her interest in living abroad. Likewise, WiSER Magi revealed how growing up in a military family influenced her. "I am a very big people person, and I think that that goes back to … growing up in the military." Given that her family often moved, she recognized the importance of making friends quickly. "It just became a part of who I was," she added. "I like being around people; I am very interested in other people's culture and the people."

Assessing your values, understanding where and how they were molded, and aligning decisions accordingly will increase confidence and reduce internal conflict. Abiding by core values serves as a compass in an ever-changing world and is evidenced in the way we go about our work. WiSER Sandra revealed that she encountered one of the darkest milestones in her career, when negative developments in the organization where she worked at the time created controversy about the business's future and growth/profit model. "At the end of the day, I think the thing I learned is, if I don't have alignment with the organization's value and what the business is trying to accomplish and why it's trying to accomplish it, it's not a great place for me to be," she said. So, once again, it all comes down to self-awareness. Although values are so integral to defining who a person is, it is not always easy to point them out and to consider them objectively. Following is a simple, yet practical approach to consider your own values.

Values exercise
1. Review the values list below, add other values if you want, and keep in mind the following: What are your favorite values? At the end of your life, how do you want to be thought of?
2. Place a star or check next to the words that resonate with you or the ones you connect with.
3. Narrow the list to 10 values.

4. Narrow the list to three. These are your top three values.
5. Prioritize them.
6. If you don't prioritize among these three values, they can conflict with each other. Let's say that two values on your list are financial independence and honesty. What if someone offers you an opportunity to earn a lot of money in a relatively short period of time? The only hitch … it may be slightly illegal although you probably won't get caught. If you have prioritized honesty over financial security, you will decline the offer.

    The bottom line … if you don't rank your values you will find yourself making decisions that may not make you happy.

Core values list		
Achievement	Privacy	Excellence
Leadership	Decisiveness	Self-respect
Advancement/promotion	Public service	Excitement
Loyalty	Democracy	Serenity
Adventure	Persistence	Physical challenge
Market position	Self-motivation	Competition
Challenging problems	Knowledge	Financial gain
Meaningful work	Humor	Personal development
Change and variety	Economic security	Competence
Money	Quality relationships	Independence
Clear communication	Effectiveness	Status
Nature	Recognition	Freedom
Close relationships	Ethical practice	Supervising others
Open and honest	Wisdom	Friendships
Cooperation	Work under pressure	Teamwork
Order	Integrity	Growth
Community	Work with others	Time freedom
Influencing others	Involvement	Helping society
Pleasure	Working alone	Truth
Creativity	Expertise	Honesty
Power and authority	Stability	Wealth
Customer service	Security	

Self-Awareness to Build Emotional Intelligence

How do you deal with challenges? How do you rally a team to achieve a goal? How do you lead? Emotional intelligence (EQ) is "the level of your ability to understand other people, what motivates them and how to work cooperatively with them" (Howard Gardner, Harvard theorist). EQ is upstaging intelligence (IQ) when it comes to achieving personal and professional success. Reading other people's signals and responding in a measured way is foundational to better understand, empathize,

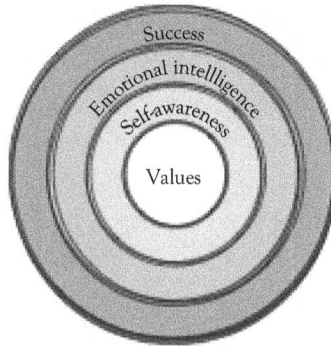

Figure 4.1 From self-awareness to success

and negotiate—particularly in a more global environment. Pressure can derail your attempts to manage your emotional approach. Therefore, it is important to be aware of what triggers you to derail your emotional response, to sustain success in your life and career. Self-awareness is foundational to emotional intelligence (Goleman 2015).

In the chaos of modern life, however, most people are unaware of their emotions. Statistics show that customer service workers and middle managers both score higher than other workers in the area of emotional intelligence. Surprisingly, C-level executives rank the lowest. Therefore, we can surmise that C-level executives are not strong in self-awareness. The good news is that everyone tends to get emotionally smarter as they grow older. The better news is that women score somewhat higher in overall emotional intelligence than men, particularly when it comes to managing relationships. The best news, however, is that we can all improve our level of emotional intelligence and self-awareness through various tools and techniques. "When you're emotionally intelligent, your emotions work for—not against—you, and you are respectful and mindful of other people's feelings" (Bradberry and Greaves 2005). Thus, EQ results in a great predictor of a person's success (Figure 4.1).

Self-Awareness to Drive Effective Decision-Making

Relying on a strong sense of self-awareness will guide difficult or challenging decision making throughout your life as you come across many interesting professional and personal opportunities. Effective decision making may include whether or not to expatriate. WiSER Argentina was young, a single mother of two, and in the middle of completing her degree when she decided to accept a position in Burundi because she enjoyed adventure, challenge, and found learning new things interesting. Her colleagues at the time commented: "Are you crazy? Those people kill each other. They have ongoing wars between the Hutus and the Tutsis." She took the risk, finished her degree while there, and the risk paid off in accelerating her career. WiSER Alicia was aware of the limitations of a dual-career marriage with the joint responsibility of raising a child, when she considered a particularly challenging job. She chose to turn down the offer. "So that's the first time I ever had to say 'no' to a job," she noted. "And I was very honest with my manager at the time, saying, 'I know my personality … I need to be able to do both well.'"

Effective decision making may impact your career decisions. "I had worked at [a financial institution] for 10 years, and that truly was a great work experience," said WiSER Alexis. "I'm very proud of many things we did there." In retrospect, however, she recognized that her decision to accept the next job was ego-driven, and the job turned out to be short-lived. "I sort of knew that company would be bought or taken over, but they offered me a lot of money, I didn't have to do any interviews, and I took that job," she recalled. "It was a stupid career decision, and I … really didn't enjoy my time there." To make matters worse, she had to deal with a scandal the bank became embroiled in, involving a $25 million fraud scheme. Remember to always rely on your international gold standard— your core values—and be acutely aware of them when navigating rocky waters.

Effective decision making will help you make tough decisions. WiSER Maxine was forced to make some ethical decisions after being given a huge task and opportunity.

> The whole idea was that, when the wall came down, when the communists had moved on, what you had was lots of people in government positions who had absolutely no management expertise, no expertise in manning organizations, because it was all about the process in those days,

she explained. "I took out teams of management trainers, teams of play therapists, teams of social workers, teams of educationalists to train up in the governments to create training institutions." The five-year program was sponsored by the European Union, and after a year-and-a-half, WiSER Maxine took the controversial decision to close it down, given that it was set up in a way that struck her as unethical. "For example, we were paying our local staff in dollars, [which was] completely unethical, so I closed it."

Effective decision making may impact work-life fit decisions, such as whether or not to have children. WiSER Claudia acknowledged: "I'm not married, and I'm not willing to have kids. Because, if I have to choose, I prefer my career—I prefer the excitement that a new challenge gives me. I prefer this liberty, this freedom to take my decisions and to choose the right way." WiSER Kamini left a high-powered position for a few years when she had children and WiSER Nathalie G. decided to work part-time. WiSER Supriya's first experience of life as an expatriate came when she followed her husband to Singapore. When she became pregnant, she had to be on "bed rest" for some time and, then, she took about two years off to spend time with her daughter—a decision that brought its share of joys but also made her realize that she really missed working. "When [my daughter] was about two, I put her into a play group and went to work part-time in research," she said. For as many mothers with young children who want to stay at home, there are just as many who want to have a space in their lives that is entirely their own. Oftentimes, work can fulfill this need.

In order to make good decisions it is important to trust your gut reaction. It often serves as an echo of your values and your sense of self. That's the advice of WiSER Jacqueline, who knew from an early age that she wanted a career that involved overseas travel. "I was the only child for six years, and my dad used to bring home ... these National Geographic magazines and Life magazine—and I used to read them from cover to cover," she recalled. "I remember when I was ... 12 years old, I said to my dad that I was going to write for [a] magazine like this, and I was going to live in Africa." She was convinced that she would write, and that she would travel in Africa, but she had no idea what she would do beyond that. As it turned out, WiSER Jacqueline's first international assignment was in Kenya. WiSER Anuradha shared with us that, at a very young age, she knew exactly what she wanted to be. She was attuned to how a very common experience inspired her. "When I was 10 years old, I was taken to the observatory in Hyderabad. I looked up and saw … what the universe has to offer … I saw … [only] six planets … but that event … solidified what I wanted to do in my life. I wanted to become an astronomer."

Self-Awareness to Boost Your Engagement

Recognizing and leveraging your personal strengths will boost your engagement resulting in increased productivity and energy, as well as improved feelings of fulfillment and competence. Being aware of your strengths also means that you understand what you are not particularly good at and are prepared to engage others with those strengths to counterbalance your own and drive results. WiSER Joanne described how she went about leveraging her strengths. "I thought I was going to be a starving artist," she revealed in the interview. "Now, I used to draw because I love to draw, and I am really good at it. I had … [an] industrial technology professor at university, and we had to design a product for his course." Although she was initially intimidated by the assignment, her professor encouraged her to build on her strengths: "He said, 'You love to draw. I watch you draw. You design things all the time. Remove all the roadblocks and just design.' This was a critical experience that prompted me into a manufacturing environment." Similarly, WiSER Lillian, who was drawn to creative writing, found a way to leverage her strength into an exciting international career. "I really liked writing a lot more than speaking in front of people," she said. "I just liked writing … but I wanted to also do something very international—and so, the one thing that [fit it] together was law." Our strengths characterize us as a person. The key to success lies in ascertaining your strengths and building on them while ensuring that your weaknesses don't become roadblocks to your success. Download the Women Leaders Toolkit from the BEP Publishing website for additional tools and resources.

Engagement not only comes from understanding and using your strengths, but also your likes. The simple calculation of multiplying the average number of 246 working days per year by 45 working years reveals that we spend about 11,000 days of our lives working, between the ages of 21 and 65. That is an enormous amount of time spent engaged in one activity. This begs an important question: What do you like doing? We can only assume that you want to spend this amount of time doing something that you actually enjoy. If you're interested in better understanding what gives you joy, download the Women Leaders Toolkit from the BEP Publishing website for additional tools and resources.

Significantly, not all of the WiSER we interviewed knew their preferred career choice early on. That said, most had a strong sense of what they liked, and what they didn't like. WiSER Gabriele indicated she had no idea where she wanted to take her career. While completing her degree in engineering in Germany, she taught evening classes at a private school. Clues to her long-term professional goals, however, were evident in her choice of recreation. During this time, she used every spare cent she had earned to travel, often to places as remote as Southeast Asia. "It was very clear [that] when I was finishing my studies that I wanted to go abroad," she said. "I said, 'If I need to work the whole day, then it must be fun, something that I really like, which is traveling.'" Meanwhile, WiSER Flavia remained steadfastly true to her interest, even though it limited her career. "If I had made different career choices throughout, I would be certainly at a much more senior level within the system," she admitted. "But I would have had to make compromises." She concluded that these compromises would have turned her position into a routine job, as opposed to an activity she found enriching and enjoyable and she refused to let that happen. "If you don't come to it with an enormous passion, it becomes very difficult. I think all my choices have been not geared to where do I make the best career choice, but what sings to me. That is important, because if you like what you do, you do it better."

In the absence of self-awareness, you may find yourself on a dangerous path that is filled with "energy zappers." WiSER Gillian recalls an experience. "I was recruited into the global role and the global CEO retired about a month after I started," she recalled. "The guy that took over from him ... We were just not a match at all." Over time, WiSER Gillian became so insecure that she dreaded going to work every morning. "I can remember how I felt," she said. "I [would] wake up in the morning, almost on the verge of tears, and it's not like me … It was [a] really, really dark moment." After a while she made up her mind and decided to leave. Just by making that decision, she started getting her confidence back. Before leaving, however, she felt a need to regain some of her lost dignity. "I went to my boss," she recalled.

> He was a board member, one of six board members. I said to him, "Look, I don't want to work with you anymore," and I told him why. … then, the global head of HR asked me not to leave and put me on some projects, and I ended up in another global role about three months later. So, I survived what I thought was a bridge burner.

Gillian's example demonstrates how important it is to know your limits and adhere to them to preserve your engagement. On the other hand, WiSER Fiona discussed some of the reasons she refrained from advancing in her career: "I realized that I didn't want to go any higher," she said.

> That was an important milestone. It's not that I have stopped working hard, or [that] I have stopped striving to do the best I can do. I could work harder to become a deputy director general; or, let's say, a director in a much larger center … but I don't want to go there, and that was sort of [a] light bulb going on for me. I know where I don't want to be in my career.

Higher engagement leads to increased safety, health, happiness, performance, and a better home life. The more engaged you are, the better you will be able to deal with the demands in your personal and professional life. You will be better at facing unfamiliar situations, dealing with uncertainties, and coping with work pressure.

The Journey to Self-Awareness

The WiSER, who demonstrated a very high level of self-awareness, shared four valuable insights to cultivating greater self-awareness.

Learn from Your Experiences

Don't discount the value of any experience, even a negative experience. All experiences can contribute to your self-awareness. WiSER Esther, for instance, described an event that she referred to as a painful learning experience. "I worked for almost five years in Liberia during the war," she recalled. "It was a very difficult time security wise … I did learn that, as a person, I am very vulnerable. I guess it was something that I needed to learn about myself." During this period, she witnessed things that she would never forget, and had no desire to witness again. Although WiSER Esther's experience was extreme, all international assignments are challenging, and they offer rare opportunities to deepen your understanding of who you are. WiSER Jolanda described the experience as follows: "All of a sudden you are put out of your comfort zone … in multiple ways, and it means you're going to learn a lot about what you like and don't like about yourself."

Look to Your Role Models to Better Understand Yourself

It is helpful to observe others you respect or admire in order to get a deeper understanding of your personal motivations. WiSER Esther described the ways in which her own upbringing and childhood role model, her father, shaped her lifelong quest for social justice. "I never met my grandparents, because [they] both died in a concentration camp," she said.

> But my father, in particular, was very strong on the issue of social justice, and perhaps this is why I ended where I ended. He taught me at a very young age that it is important to remember that all human beings are equal, that social justice comes before anything else.

She ended up working in social relief organizations.

Harness Introspection

Have you reached the top of the ladder and found that maybe it's leaning against the wrong building? In some cases, you may find that you need personal time to make decisions about your future. WiSER Ayesha had reached a stage where she was no longer stimulated by her professional career. At some point, she decided that she wanted something that was "far more noble, far more exciting, and far more challenging and pioneering." Recognizing that her current path was no longer viable, she began to consider alternatives. "Can I put other steps into place?" she asked herself. "Or do I just make a clean break now and spend some time deciding what the next step in my life should be?" Ultimately, she decided to take some time off and make some clear decisions about her future. In some cases, a change of scenery can be helpful. WiSER Friederike left for India to do some serious introspection. She knew that she enjoyed working with people and liked networking. "But I also need to know who I am," she added.

Engage the Help of a Coach

A coach is a trusted professional who can support you to identify your professional needs and goals, develop a plan of action, and achieve results. WiSER Anne related her experience with a coach. Fearful that she would remain with the same organization for the remainder of her professional life, WiSER Anne found that her coach helped her imagine other possibilities. "I think, really, what helped me make that change was, when I got back to the states, I got a coach," she said. "She helped me go through a lot of kind of imagining new possibilities for … the future—something I [had] never really done. She kept saying, well that could be good, that might happen, so what else could happen?" she recalled. "I think it was just visualizing different things."

It's a Wrap!

As Lao-Tzu wisely said: "It is wisdom to know others, it is enlightenment to know one's self." In an international role, the complexities involved demand an even greater sense of self-awareness. Being self-aware involves knowing your strengths and weaknesses, your likes and dislikes, which are all based on your values. Self-awareness is the basis of emotional intelligence, effective decision making, and engagement. Being

self-aware increases emotional intelligence. In an international environment, this is particularly helpful to work effectively with others to drive
results and make good decisions in critical situations. You can increase
your self-awareness by learning from experiences, looking to your role
models, being introspective, and working with a coach. If only the queen
in "Snow White" had possessed a greater sense of self-awareness and taken
the time to understand the reflection in the mirror, the story might have
ended differently. Your story, however, has yet to be written.

CHAPTER 5

Conscious Imbalance

Life is like riding a bicycle. To keep your [im]balance you must keep moving.

—*Adapted from Albert Einstein*

I decided to throw the word "balance" out of my life ... Balance suggests this sort of stable, level [scale] where one side equals the other. In my philosophy ... life is very dynamic and it's always moving, so ... things never stay the same. So, I call it managing the dynamics, as opposed to balance.

—*WiSER Abby*

Balance is defined as an even distribution of weight that enables someone—or something—to remain upright and steady. Have you ever tried to maintain perfect balance in your life? If so, how long did you manage to maintain it? What, or who, did you say "no" to in order to maintain it? Did you achieve an authentic balance, in which the scales of your personal and professional lives were perfectly even, or was it that you spent more time tilting the scales, calling it balance because it felt right to you? Balance is like the holy grail, compelling and elusive at best. WiSER Flavia described some of the challenges involved in attempting to "balance" professional and personal responsibilities. "I'm very conscious that there is a stress element. ... Women are good at having—a tendency to always feel that they fall short," WiSER Flavia added. "I think I've come to terms with that, in the sense that we can't be perfect and there will be some degree of imperfection—both professionally and personally." She noted that her professional work has led her to rethink the unrealistic standards she imposed on herself. "In development, we've been very engaged in promoting governance in countries where we work," she explained. "A few years ago, the UK Department of Development [told us] we shouldn't go for perfection. We should look for good enough governance, and I think we need to look for 'good enough' balance as well."

We recommend tipping the scales to target them toward your strongest moments resulting in a fulfilling life. Dozens of WiSER have chosen to live their lives this way, and they have found tremendous success and happiness in the process of practicing conscious imbalance. This should not leave you riddled with guilt. "When the children [were] younger, I [felt] that I just ran my life by guilt," WiSER Alexis recalled. "I constantly felt guilty for not being at work, or guilty for not being at home when the children were sick or … I missed some important event at school." Despite such challenges, however, she added, "I would do it all again— five times over." Dan Thurmon (2010), author and motivational speaker on the topic of living off-balance, describes it as living life intentionally off-balance for a specific purpose.

A Positive Definition

Imbalance is often regarded as an undesirable condition. The common view is that someone in an imbalanced situation has not chosen his/her lot. However, this isn't always the case. You may perceive others' life as imbalanced and think that as a result they must be unhappy. However, if their situation is the result of conscious, deliberate choices which fulfills them, the perception is actually inaccurate. Imbalance can result from the fact that choices are made to either spend most of one's time devoted to career or devoted to personal priorities such as family. For WiSER Martine, the term "work-life balance" is misleading. "It's not about work-life balance; it's about being satisfied in both—or multiple—aspects of your life. It shows. If you are frustrated at home and you are not having a good time, it's going to spill over into your work." And if your work is frustrating, your personal life and relations will suffer as a result of it.

People are searching for deeply satisfying personal and professional lives, not a balance or compromise between the two. Often there are competing priorities, and we need to understand which way we want to tip the scales in order to achieve deeper fulfillment. When Matthew Kelly, author of *Off Balance*, conducted interviews, he found that responses to his questions about people's most satisfying periods involved descriptions of extreme situations. They were stories about putting in 70 hours per week for a few months in order to deliver a high-profile project on time and under budget. Or, they were stories of sitting on the beach in the Bahamas doing nothing more than sipping on a Pina Colada. They were rarely stories about working on the beach, for instance, which would reflect the proverbial balance.

Conscious imbalance, the idea of tipping the scales as a conscious, deliberate choice in order to feel fully satisfied is about adapting to ever changing situations rather than maintaining a status quo. It is embracing what might be versus protecting what is, choosing growth over stagnation, and having more of what truly matters versus having a little of everything (Thurmon 2010). For the purpose of our research, we defined the competency "Conscious imbalance" as follows:

Conscious imbalance
Tipping the scales toward what gives you energy and fulfillment with the realization that the scales will need to be rebalanced on a regular basis.
• You set your own priorities regardless of standards or others' opinions. • You create or maintain a conscious imbalance between professional and personal life. • You determine when one must dominate the other. • You get what you want from both priorities.

Half of WiSER (50 percent) demonstrated these skills. Interestingly, if we examine types of organization, women working for governmental organizations demonstrated this competency far more than the others: 88 percent compared to 49 percent of women in for-profit organizations and 38 percent of women in non-profit organizations. Women from North America demonstrated this competency at a comparatively higher rate (57 percent) than women from Europe (44 percent).

On the spectrum of conscious imbalance, where do you think you fall? Where would you like to be? What steps can you take to get there?

Imbalanced ◄——————— **CONSCIOUS IMBALANCE** ———————► Perfection

Considering that we were talking to WiSER, many of our interviewees were inclined to tip the scales in the direction of work, projects, and travel. When you talk about men tipping the scales toward work, it is considered normal, and it is certainly regarded as acceptable. However, when a woman does this, it is often questioned. "How could you be happy doing this?" As WiSER Faith told us:

> I think that when you love what you do, it gets really hard to know what this whole work-life balance is, because it doesn't always feel like work to me. Other people, like my partner, need to remind me. I'll never forget the night, at around 3 O'clock in the morning, he got up to go to the bathroom and he found me. The whole house is dark. I'm sitting in my nightgown, with my face blue, glowing from my Blackberry. He said, "What are you doing? Why are you online? Come back to sleep." I responded, "Yeah, yeah, yeah." Clearly that's not healthy, but I loved what I was into.

Interestingly, some of the women who discussed with us their efforts to maintain a work-life balance revealed choices that in fact demonstrated conscious imbalance. The overall message is best said in the words of Madeleine Albright: "women can have it all, just not at the same time." Thoughtful concessions based on priorities will have to be made. WiSER Britta draws from her personal experience when discussing this phenomenon. "You have to go after what you want, when it is the right time for you," she advised. "People have criticized me for wanting it all—child and family and living abroad and ambitious career." She added that many people have recommended that she scale down her commitments and her aspirations. "I think it is important to accept when you have a demanding job and a child or family, there is no balance—forget it," she said. "Prioritize and outsource things like house cleaning, lawn care, and other low-priority items in order to spend your time on high-priority, high-value things."

The WiSER discussed with us many situations in which they had to give something up in order to meet their goals. Giving something up is not easy. They indicated, however, that, in the long run, the sacrifice was worth it. WiSER Anuradha found that consciously imbalancing her personal and professional life required her and her husband to live in separate locations. While she lived in India, her husband resided in the

United States. "My husband went off because he got a big job offer, and I was not ready to give up this wonderful thing that I … had worked so hard for," she explained.

> We lived for three years with our firstborn in two separate households. We worked very hard to meet every six weeks for a week. I had a lot of support from my parents. Six months the baby stayed with his father; six months he stayed with his mom … He spent his first four years traveling back and forth and had more frequent flyer miles than I did.

As their son grew older, however, WiSER Anuradha and her husband concluded that the arrangement was no longer viable, and she made the decision to move closer to her husband. Similarly, WiSER Ulrike, who has a partner, decided on a long-distance relationship for professional reasons. When she received an assignment in Finland, he chose to remain in Germany. "We don't have kids," she explained. "So, in that respect, it was quite easy." They would meet twice a month.

When making concessions, however, it is not always tipped toward professional commitments. Many WiSER have given up on a great career opportunity to the benefit of their family. WiSER Veronika chose not to accept a position because of her familial responsibilities. "There was a time when I could have gotten a better job in my company being responsible for many more people," she revealed. "But I decided to say, 'no,' because it really didn't fit into my family life." Similarly, WiSER Britta had to give up on some of her favorite pastimes. "You … need to prioritize and aim for self-fulfillment, while realizing that you will have to give some things up. Yoga classes, retreats … are not part of my life," she acknowledged. "Do I miss it? Yes. But I am prioritizing."

Regardless of how you tip the scales, or which priorities you set, it is essential to take time for yourself. When life is going at a hundred miles an hour, you might forget to look after yourself. Even if you spend 18 hours a day doing what you love doing, you still need time to relax, reload, and take your mind off things. "I think that, because of the stress and the time that goes into the job, you have to be aware of it and you have to really plan some time for yourself, some time to reflect, time to relax, because if you don't consciously plan it, you won't have it," advised WiSER Elsa L. "The job will wear you out." If you don't manage your life purposefully, you won't have time for yourself.

One of the WiSER shared a story about a female colleague who worked hard and long, traveled the world, and was constantly training for the next marathon. Much to her embarrassment, she passed out on the shop floor after arriving for a meeting. Similarly, another one of the WiSER, Karin, found her job to be a dangerously exhausting experience. "I was actually working so much that … I had to find another job," she recalled. "And, I wasn't able to … know or feel within myself when enough was enough. So, I was working seven days a week, 10 to 12 hours a day to keep up with the projects." She added that it took her a couple of years to recover from this experience. "So, in a way, you could say that I almost got killed by my own success because I wasn't able to stop," she added.

As we mentioned, the scales of your life will need to be re-calibrated on a regular basis. This means that, over time, you may desire to spend more time on personal commitments—or after devoting a good deal of time to such priorities, you may wish to have a renewed focus on professional commitments. "I made the choice to be a single mom and I adopted my daughter," WiSER Janice revealed. "And when I made that choice, I kind of took a step back in my career for two years, and I took a role … with a … good title, and I got paid very well, but … I had no professional. I made that decision because I had adopted my baby girl." Similarly, WiSER Nathalie G. made some changes in response to the demands of raising a family. "When our first son was born, I had a quiet phase for 24 months," she said. This meant little traveling and working part-time. "And then, I took on the global strategic marketing role, and I was traveling again to the US, China, and to India."

After many years of being a WiSER with a trailing spouse, WiSER Laura tipped her scales completely to the other side to support her husband's professional goals, even though her career was actually more lucrative. "We made the conscious decision that my husband deserves a chance. He has a master's degree. He has a lot to give to students." While she was confident she could do her job extremely well, she indicated: "We did make the conscious decision to make that switch, which involved a lot of sacrifice as well … but … in a good sort of way."

How to Achieve Conscious Imbalance—Tips

"There is no secret to balance; you just have to feel the waves." Frank Herbert. Successful surfers must develop a feel for where their body is positioned relative to the flow of the waves. They do this by keeping their eyes on the horizon, looking ahead and never down. They have trained their body's muscle memory to instinctually tense and release muscles at the right times and in just the right increments allowing them to stay on the board. In female expatriate terms: you have to constantly recalibrate and reassess your priorities to remain content. WiSER demonstrated time and time again how they have imbalanced their lives in order to do what gives them energy and happiness. Download the Women Leaders Toolkit from the BEP Publishing website for additional tools and resources.

Off balance exercises are important to strengthen your core muscles. Equipment such as a yoga ball, forces you off balance, therefore requiring you to use your core muscles more frequently. As you enter your expatriate experience, conscious imbalance can strengthen you at the core in order to perform optimally in your new role. Here are some off balance practices shared by WiSER.

Don't Let Societal Expectations Dictate Your Priorities

One of the most important messages the WiSER imparted was the importance of going after your dreams. Don't give up on your goals because of other people's attitudes toward you, your lifestyle, and your choices. What may work for you does not necessarily conform with other people's values and practices—and vice versa. "I love my work, and I couldn't live without work," WiSER Maria revealed. "Balance is a very personal thing. Probably, when friends of mine would look at my life, they would think I am not at all in balance. Well, I am fine with it. It all depends on what your priorities are, obviously."

The WiSER stressed that there is no need to give up on your dreams as your life evolves. Our women demonstrate that it is possible to have a wonderful international career, solo, along with a partner, and/or a family. It may not always be easy, but if your goal is to move abroad, you should attempt to realize your ambitions. In the end, all that matters is that you are happy with your own life, and how you lead it. All the women whose personal scales tipped in the direction of work loved what they were doing. They enjoyed their work so they did not view spending less time in other areas as an unreasonable sacrifice. It was their deliberate choice, which led to happiness and fulfillment.

Validate the Needs of Your Family and Employer

Although you may be open to the idea of doing more of the things you enjoy, chances are that you will also be concerned about tipping the scales in such a way that you risk letting down either your employer or your family. Therefore, it is important to get a clear understanding of their expectations of you. By this we mean that you have to really know what they expect as opposed to you presuming to know what they expect. A fascinating study cited by Marcus Buckingham may shed light on this subject. The study involved more than one thousand young people in the United States between the grades of three to 12. The participants were asked this question: "If you were granted one wish that would change the way that your mother's/your father's work affects your life, what would that wish be?" In a parallel study, more than six hundred employed mothers and fathers were asked to guess how their children would respond to this question. Here's what they found:

> Most parents (56 percent) guessed that their children would wish for more time with them. But "more time" was not at the top of children's wish list. Only 10 percent of children made that wish about their mothers and 15.5 percent about their fathers. Most children wished that their mothers (34 percent) and their fathers (27.5 percent) would be less stressed and tired. (Buckingham 2009, p. 228)

In other words, kids want parents to be happier, not necessarily to spend more time with them.

Call in the Troops

No one can do it all by themselves, nor should anyone be expected to do so. This is why it is so important to build up a support network on international assignments within a short period of time. "While living in South Africa, I hired a full-time nanny and was also backed by my family and friends," said WiSER Erica, who is a single mother.

> In Australia my kids were a little older, but I had a housekeeper that helped me with basics, such as cleaning the house, ensuring the laundry was done, ensuring that the kids got fed when they came back from school and then in the evenings I would cook and enjoy time with my boys.

She added that her support structure included a strong network of friends, whom she didn't hesitate to contact when she needed assistance.

Most of the WiSER who were married indicated their spouses played a critical role in their professional success, given that they provided constant support, encouragement, and assistance. "It is difficult to balance the two," WiSER Lillian observed, when describing her efforts to maintain professional and personal responsibilities. "It's not a very steady balance because there are moments ... where sometimes work gets priority, and there are moments ... where the family gets the priority." She noted that her husband is extremely supportive of her professional goals. "Definitely, without him being as involved as he is at home, it would be much more difficult than what it is," she said. "But I never wanted the fact that we had children to stop me." Interestingly, WiSER Abby had a similar story to tell. "My husband has always been really, really supportive and comfortable," she revealed. "That meant that sometimes he would do more stuff with the kids' school than me." She added that her husband often spends more time with the children on weekends as well, because her job requires her to travel.

Advocate for What You Need

A number of WiSER indicated that the best policy is to be open with employers about your needs and desires to either take on an international assignment, a big project, or to "be there" for personal commitments. Requests for time off to address these needs are usually granted without any problems. WiSER Erica noted, "I think it is crucial that you communicate clearly with your manager and when they cut you some slack, you need to make sure you get your work done on time and with high quality." She added that if you do so, you will generate trust and credibility, which is vital for managing multiple priorities. International assignments will be demanding. Being honest and advocating for what you require to be successful may afford you extra flexibility to tip the scales.

It's a Wrap!

We have but one life, and we withdraw time from the same time bank, which provides 24 hours a day, spread over 365 days a year. We aren't simply trying to balance, say, a cup of "work" and a cup of "personal life." We are looking at one cup that is brimming with who we are, and we don't want anything valuable to spill out.

Never stop thinking about the moments in your life that have brought you great joy and fulfillment. Once you understand that, you can make the hard choices that are involved in tipping the scales—and lead a more fulfilling life. The WiSER suggest working on conscious imbalance by making choices based on your goals rather than societal expectations; validating the needs of your family and employer rather than assuming you know what they need or want; and, ask for the support you require both personally and professionally, rather than suffering in silence. As you pass through different phases in life, the scales may be tipped differently, so it's necessary to calibrate them on a regular basis. Adopting a conscious attitude of imbalance means that you are tipping the scales of personal and professional demands according to your key priorities and personal standards.

As WiSER Marieke sums it up: "I've heard many women beating themselves down, although they are doing a great, excellent job managing both professional and personal lives. What we have to work on is believing in ourselves."

CHAPTER 6

Active Career Management

Think not of yourself as the architect of your career but as the sculptor. Expect to have to do a lot of hard hammering and chiseling and scraping and polishing.

—B.C. Forbes

Life is short, life is yours, don't rely on someone else to make your dreams come true.

—WiSER Faith

Think back on your most recent vacation. When you took that vacation, did you simply jump in your car and start driving, with no hotel bookings, no map, no GPS, no intended destination, and no plan in mind whatsoever? If you've ever done this, you are more adventurous than most people. That said, if you understand the basic parameters of your vacation you will reduce travel time and stress, and get to your intended destination more efficiently. Taking an expatriate assignment is a similar proposition in the sense that advance planning will position you to leverage your international experience in order to accelerate your career. If you start with the end in mind, active career management is the map to your destination. It is a very significant and specific process that can yield tremendous professional return. Remember, you cannot throw a dart and call whatever it hits the bullseye.

We defined the competency of "Active career management" as:

Active career management
Knowing what you want from your career and working with intention to achieve those goals.
• You make things happen for yourself and pursue your professional interests regardless of geography, profession, or field. • You are able to influence and shape the decisions of upper management.

- You market yourself and don't wait for others to open doors.
- You proactively manage a network to reach career goals by winning support from others.
- You actively learn and develop yourself.
- You welcome solicited and unsolicited feedback and modify your behavior in light of it.

Two-thirds (66 percent) of the WiSER we interviewed had actively managed their careers, and they indicated this played an important role in their rise to a senior-level expatriate role. Among those who did not actively manage their careers, the majority recommended that others should. Those WiSER who demonstrated the competency of self-aware-ness, also demonstrated active career management to a greater extent (69 percent) than those who did not explicitly demonstrate self-aware-ness (55 percent). The presence of conscious imbalance was greater among women who did not actively manage their careers (62 percent) than among those who did (41 percent). Interestingly, WiSER who had self-initiated their expatriation had been less active in managing their career (57 percent) than women who had been sent abroad by their orga-nization (70 percent). We attribute this to the fact that when working in an organization, there are more barriers to overcome in order to be considered for an international assignment. An early desire to live abroad did not have an effect on this competency, neither did the type of organi-zation the WiSER worked for.

On the spectrum of active career management, where do you think you fall? Where would you like to be? What steps can you take to get there?

No Plan ◄——— **PLAN WITH ROOM FOR FLEXIBILITY** ———► Over-Architected Plan

Research has indicated that the younger you move abroad, the more it benefits your career (Reiche 2011). In line with this conclusion, the majority of the women we interviewed (60 percent) were junior professionals when they first expatriated. That said, if you haven't been abroad before a certain age, it doesn't mean your chances are over. We have spoken with WiSER who began their international career after more than 20 years of experience in multiple organizations, and they went on to land great jobs.

Let's revisit the analogy we began with—your vacation. At this point, you have defined your destination (an expatriate role) and mapped out your route (what actions will get you there). Now, think about finding some friends to include on your journey. These friends may include someone who clarifies where the GPS is directing you, helps you refuel, or someone who occasionally takes over the driving. In career management terms, these friends comprise your network, which consists of mentors and sponsors—influential people who know you and recognize your value. Talent management decisions, including the selection of expatriates, are usually made with the input of many people, and information is passed through formal, as well as informal channels. One of the most common reasons for not achieving a goal is that we don't seek the support needed to achieve it. WiSER Julie Anne learned the importance of having a network of supporters early in her career. "In the first years of my career, I thought that, if I worked hard and was better than my peers ... I would be successful and rewarded with additional responsibilities," she stated. "I learned over time that those traits are only the price of entry ... but that it's not enough to achieve what you want."

While women have always been recognized as natural relationship builders, their networks in professional arenas are generally not as strong as those maintained by men. Our research revealed that 58 percent do not have a group of trusted advisors, and 40 percent lack supportive relationships in their professional life. There are many reasons for this phenomenon, but we will only focus on couple of them. First, many professions still harbor "old-boy networks," which systematically exclude women. Second, women often have more after-work responsibilities, and these tend to limit their opportunities to network beyond the office. Whatever the reasons, it is important to remember that networks are invaluable, given that they serve as channels to learn a wide range of information from what is going on in your organization, your industry, and possibly even learn about new opportunities, including the availability of international opportunities.

Characteristics of a Strong Network

Strong, impactful networks are interwoven, diverse (in terms of industry, function, age, gender, and geography), and well nurtured. As per Rob

Cross, UVA professor and expert in social networking, "Your network determines, in part, the size of your paycheck" (Cross, Cowen, Vertucci, and Thomas 2012, p. 4). Women tend to compartmentalize personal, professional, external, internal, and client networks rather than blurring the lines between them which could lead to more impactful networks and occasionally provide unexpected opportunities. WiSER Annette recalled that, during a trip to New York City to visit with friends, she happened to run into a former co-worker at her previous company. "We started chatting, and he invited me to come to a party that he was having that evening" she explained. "I went along to that party, and I was talking to him and another guy there, and they had just left their previous firm to go and work at a global media organization, and they were setting up a project team to do all of the big changes associated with early digital music." WiSER Annette noted that this was before the advent of the iPod, and the project team was going to be involved in a whole array of change projects. "And they basically said to me, 'We're looking for change managers to come and join our group. If you fancy it, the job is yours,' and I was blown away!" She explained that she had always loved music, and therefore, she jumped at the chance to work in the music industry. "It was important to me because it made me realize … that a lot of being successful at what you do is about the relationship and the network, rather than actually what you know," she said. "I think there is a tipping point in your career where you know almost as much as the next person, and where people are making a decision about whether they want to work with you based on whether they like your personality or not, whether they know you—rather than a decision based on what you know."

Women are more than five times likely to rely on a network that is mostly female. There are benefits to formal women's networks. Women's networks were found to be effective, an incredible way to engage women, and beneficial to career development. Notably, research showed that women who went to a women's conference were twice as likely to receive a promotion and three times as likely to receive at least a 10 percent pay increase (Achor 2018). However, women cannot afford to limit themselves to either formal or informal networks primarily comprised of women. Men typically hold more senior-level positions, which means that women who rely on women-only networks are less likely to get access to and visibility among people who can open doors for them. The power dynamics in the professional ranks statistically favor men, from 77 percent of U.S. Congress to 95 percent of Fortune 500 CEO titles. "It's men and boys (soon to be men) in the driver's seat. It's men who are obligated to help create change" (Lui 2014).

If you are interested in getting a gut check of your networking skills, your NQ, answer the following questions. These questions will help you better understand the scope and strength of your network. This assessment is adapted from The Connect Effect by networking expert Michael Dulworth (2008).

Networking IQ assessment
1. How many total people are in your personal, professional, and virtual networks?
2. How strong are your relationships with the people in your network?
3. How diverse is your network?
4. What is the overall quality of your network contacts?
5. To what extent do you actively work on building your network relationships?
6. How often do you actively recruit new members to your network?
7. How often do you help others in your network?
8. To what extent do you leverage technology (social media and apps) to build and maintain your networks?

It is important to build and maintain your network before you actually need it. It takes a lot of time and energy to build a network. You have to get people to notice you, like you, trust you, value you, and believe in you. Only then will they speak up for you when important decisions are made. If you wait to build connections until you need them, it will be too late. "There are more than a dozen people that have had a big impact on my career," revealed WiSER Sandra. "I always talk about being successful in terms of the content of the work you do and the contacts you make and how you work with other people." She added that she has remained in touch with many professional contacts over the past 20 or 30 years. "I have been able to maintain lasting relationships with them," she added, noting that this task, while not easy, is well worth the effort.

Strategic Networking

Strategic networking entails targeting and cultivating relationships that can bring a range of knowledge, skills, and abilities which are aligned with your professional goals. These relationships can be formal or informal, inside or outside your organization, peers or managers. Strategic networks will include mentors, sponsors, allies, connectors, industry experts, and possibly a personal Board. The majority of the WiSER (85 percent) cited having had one or more sponsors and/or mentors. Review your network to identify gaps and determine where you want to spend your efforts to develop strong, targeted, and strategic relationships.

As WiSER Julie Anne rose to the level of middle management, she found it increasingly challenging to move higher. She described some of her strategic networking efforts to move ahead. She noted that her success in getting a network of key supporters depended, to a large extent, on conscious planning. She put together a heatmap that included the names of everyone in her organization that could potentially help her advance in her career. "It included managers for other functions, managers that I hadn't worked with in years, managers that were around me now, previous managers," she explained. "You name it, I had it on the list." She kept these contacts informed on a regular basis regarding her activities and achievements, thereby giving herself positive and frequent exposure. This not only positioned her to demonstrate her range of skills, but it also ensured that she would be on their minds constantly. This strategy proved effective, where hard work alone had failed. "Part of the reason I almost left the company is that I didn't have a sponsor," she recalled. "There was no one fighting for me. You know, you can be a hard worker and you can deliver excellent work; you can be better than your peers. But if you don't have key decision makers supporting you actively and sponsoring you, it is lucky if you get what you want in your career." She concluded: "I garnered my first supporters in 2000, and they were the ones that were with me until the day I left the organization in 2010 ... That's what I did, and that's what worked."

The Importance of Mentors—A Sounding Board

A mentor typically helps you develop your skills and competencies, acts as a sounding board, and gives you general feedback and career advice. Mentors support you in a practical sense. They are people with whom you have a more interactive and personal relationship. Thus, they are able to give you insights about yourself, and provide sound career advice.

WiSER Hanan shared her experiences regarding a mentor who helped make a positive difference in her career. "I had a mentor, and he pushed me," she recalled. "He pushed my boundaries. He had confidence in me, and he pushed me … to the next level." Her mentor did not just offer encouragement and advice, she noted, but he also continually challenged her. "He would say, 'Don't come to me with a problem; come to me with a solution,'" she said. "So, he started to prepare me for business problem solving, and … what general managers were looking for." This helped her to understand that she would need to work hard and be totally committed to achieve her goals.

A mentor can also help you put things in perspective. "In every job that I have been in, I have been very fortunate to … have a relationship with someone whose input has value," related WiSER Hermie. "So, it's not like I have had one mentor consistently through my career, but I think at least three people." We recommend developing a series of mentor relationships, rather than depending on a single individual, in order to get different types of advice and support depending on the situation and your need.

In some cases, a mentor will actively cultivate a mentee. This was true of WiSER Argentina's mentor. "He would go out of his way to open the space to let me be, let me shine, and put my potential out there like never before," she recalled. WiSER Fiona described one mentor who proved to be an invaluable sounding board for her. They had met when she was first assigned to Kenya, and they developed an excellent rapport. "She was a French woman who was the head of HR," she recalled. "We became friends, and when I left Kenya, she went to Hong Kong and went from working with an NGO—working with the poor and the hungry in Africa—to being an executive for Louis Vuitton in France." WiSER Fiona kept in touch with her former colleague over the years and gained a perspective on issues that she wouldn't have gained by talking to someone in her own sector. "She's always been a great sounding board for me because she understands the systems, yet she stands outside of it and works in a totally different field," she explained.

> Every once in a while, when she starts going on about the prices of Louis Vuitton handbags and how she can get people to increase sales figures to billions … I start saying to her … "Well, yes I'm

dealing with people that have less than a dollar a day and can't educate their children."

She added: "It's great that we can do that with each other. I understand the world in a much more balanced way."

The Importance of Sponsors—Career Advancers

Sponsors are often confused with mentors, but the difference is significant. Bear in mind that one person can serve the role of both mentor and sponsor. Unlike mentors, sponsors serve as important advocates within the organization and can help you move your career forward. Sponsorship involves the active support of a well-placed individual within the organization who is involved in decision-making and acts to promote or protect the career advancement of an individual. As you advance to senior levels, sponsorship becomes increasingly important, given that you are "fighting" for scarce positions. A sponsor can propel you to the top of a list of candidates, thus immensely increasing your chances of getting your dream job. Sponsors can give you access to powerful networks, something that women have far less access to than men. It is one of the key reasons that women are underrepresented in executive positions. A sponsor can also prepare you for the complexities of new roles or assignments, help you develop skills that support advancement, and help you gain visibility (Foust-Cummings, Dinolfo, and Kohler 2011).

In many cases, a sponsor can help you "buck the odds." WiSER Alicia shared a particularly touching story about a manager who made a crucial difference in her career. "One thing I kept in my career is handwritten notes from what I consider one of my best managers," she said. "He took a big chance on me early on." After recognizing WiSER Alicia's talents, he pulled her from a number of co-op assignments and gave her a job that involved real responsibility. "He gave me a very big managerial assignment, very young," she recalled. "I ran a 100-person, all-male machine shop when I was 23. Of all three shifts, I was the only salaried person. Everyone else was hourly, and I had two hourly technical representatives." As the only woman manager, she immediately faced resistance. "I had people, right away, come up to me and say, 'I don't want a woman in the job,'" she said. Her manager, who was an African American man had worked up the managerial ladder and had dealt with racial prejudice in the course of his own career. With a personal understanding of such challenges, he was highly supportive. "He used to write me handwritten notes such as 'Hey Alicia, these are the things that you really need to focus on; you can't change the world, focus on these activities, choose your battles,'" she recalled. Although she worked for this manager for less than three years, she kept all of these letters of encouragement. "When I heard he was retiring, I flew back, went to his retirement party, pulled out my little cards, and read them, and brought him to tears," she said. "But he was one of those pivotal people that took a big chance on me and guided me, when no one else would have taken that risk." WiSER Alicia indicated that she pays it forward with younger colleagues. "I try to do the same and take chances on people, take risks on people, all while giving them the hard feedback," she said.

WiSER Maria noted that her first expatriate role owed much to the intervention of a sponsor. "You need people in the company that know you and that would support you," she said. "My sponsor knew that Canada had to get a new Director. He knew that I was looking." She added that her sponsor approached those who were recruiting for the position and strongly recommended her for the job. "They weren't aware, actually, that I was looking for a job," she said. "But he told them, and then they immediately jumped on it and came to me." Significantly, effective sponsors can help you to overcome barriers, to plug into a larger professional network, and to promote you. They can also help you navigate the political environment that is inherent in any large organization.

The Importance of Allies

Women for Women

Identifying a good sponsor or mentor is just as important as being a good sponsor or mentor to others, especially in the case of women due to the relatively small percentage of women in expatriate and leadership roles. Notably, close to 40 percent of WiSER said they had a female mentor. As international female leaders, they shared some of the ways in which they benefited from coaching and mentorship. Many of them also described how, after moving into senior level positions, they attempted to stay in the line of sight and serve as role models for young women, encouraging and supporting them in their efforts to build an international career. "I think other women can really help women and encourage them and to kind of fight so they get heard and they get considered," WiSER Martha stated.

> I was really fortunate in that respect, as I had a colleague … that was willing to do that for me. So, maybe, as women, we have a role to play in terms of seeing that potential, and really encouraging women to go after leadership positions and to aspire to those positions.

She stated that such support is essential because men are more likely than women to envision themselves in such roles. "So, maybe," she said "we need other women to come alongside and say, 'Hey, you can do it, I believe in you. Go for it.'"

WiSER Martha revealed that she knew some strong women leaders who encouraged her to apply for an expatriate assignment, and who supported her when she was pregnant. "During the application process, I actually found out I was pregnant with our second child," she recalled. "So, I wrote this long email saying that I was going to have to withdraw my application, because their Mozambique program was really big." She explained that the $25-million program covered five provinces and involved 900 staff members. In addition to being pregnant, WiSER Martha was just 33 years old. "So, I said, 'Look, there is no way the organization should want me to do this because I just found out that I am pregnant,'" she recalled.

> I still remember my sponsor marching into my office and saying: "No way! You need to put your name back in. Women have babies. Just tell them what sort of support you need. Africa is a great place to raise a family. You can do it."

Women-for-women will result in more progressive work environments, where women are well represented in leadership and expatriate roles. Some WiSER have gone so far as to recommend the benefits of female-to-female mentoring relationships. "I think that with female mentors you can … be more transparent … and not feel as guarded," said WiSER Elsa I. At one point in her career, WiSER Nathalie G. decided to seek out a female mentor who had more children than she did, and she managed to find one. "There was an American lady working in the US, and she has four children, and she is doing fine," she said. "She has made a great career for herself in our organization." She added, "It was very helpful to me to be able to talk with another woman, and I had only one child at that time." This experience was so positive that it has inspired WiSER Nathalie G. to mentor younger female colleagues.

Male Allies

When the ocean waters rise, everyone is raised to a higher level. One of the biggest misconceptions about gender equality is the sole focus on benefitting women, while the actual goal is to make positive changes that will benefit both men and women. The goal is to attract and prepare diverse talent to build robust talent pipelines resulting in positive organizational impact. Men reaching back to pull women forward is a key tenant to achieving the goal. Yet not all men want to reach back. Fear of attracting other men's disapproval and apathy are the main barriers preventing men from actively supporting gender equality (De Paula 2016). Men can actively support gender equality by avoiding gender (or any other form of) discrimination and minimizing implicit gender bias. Being a male ally is not a noun, it's a verb. Often, men are left wondering what more they can do, and women struggle with delineating actions. Following is a short list of actions men can take to become an impactful male ally, which will result in diverse pipelines and benefit the organization as a whole.

- *Transform workplace behavior.* Men can contribute to transforming the workplace culture by making it easier to openly support women. This can be done by relatively simple actions, such as including diversity topics in meetings, and drawing attention to the diversity of candidate slates. Taking a chance also includes that men call out injustices, even if they don't impact them. For example, when a colleague calls a woman "aggressive" or worse, they can explain how that same behavior is often described as being "assertive" if demonstrated by a man. In fact, being assertive is often considered an important skill for leaders. If women are the ones asked to get coffee or take notes in every meeting, men can question the practice or volunteer themselves.

- *Advocate for women.* When men continue to be the "dominant voice" in the room, it limits the chances of creating an inclusive environment, where diverse ideas are shared. Male allies can seek ways for female employees to be better seen, heard, and recognized. If you manage a team, ask women to present and lead projects. Build professional relationships with, mentor, or sponsor diverse talent in the organization. WiSER Karin encountered one of her most effective mentors after joining a Big Four consulting firm. "He is the best salesperson I have ever met in my life, and I respect him a lot and he has become a very, very good friend," she said. "I think it's the similar pattern ... he trusted me more than I did. So, he persuaded me to take a role in management consulting and to take the bigger roles abroad." At one point, her mentor encouraged her to give a presentation in Spain, where the 200 guests included influential professionals from some of Europe's largest companies. "He put his trust in me," she recalled. "So, I thought, 'If he says I can do it, I can do it,' and then I just did."

- *Provide constructive criticism.* Research shows that "women are more than 20 percent less likely than men to receive difficult feedback that helps improve their performance" (Luxton 2016). Both male and female managers are reluctant to do this because they fear sounding harsh. They are less concerned that this will be happen when giving feedback to male employees. Women are systematically less likely to receive feedback tied to outcomes. Fostering a culture of feedback, by giving honest and fair feedback, allows all employees to get a better idea of how they are performing. It acclimates everyone with how to give and receive positive and constructive feedback and how to deal with it (Correll 2016).

- *Don't "Manterrupt."* Research shows that men interrupt women in conversations far more often than they interrupt other men. Likewise, women get less credit for their contributions than men. Yale professor Victoria L. Brescoll's study found that women not only speak less often than men in meetings, but also when male executives speak more than their peers, they are rewarded with 10 percent higher competence ratings. When female executives speak more than their peers, both men and women give them 14 percent lower ratings (Center for Women and Business 2017). As a male ally, listen actively, and when you hear a woman being interrupted, find the opportunity to redirect the conversation back her way.

Some of these actions are simple, others might require more effort. Even small changes in individual behavior have the potential to make a positive difference in talent pipelines and create a more inclusive work environment. As shared by HR executive, Tony,

In the annual U.S. NFL (National Football League) draft-pick, the team with the worst season record gets the first pick in order to improve their team standing. In corporate terms, let's say the top "draft pick" happens to be a woman. However, she declines your offer because she wants to go to another team where she believes she will be played more and find the support she desires. Then your team can go further down the list of draft picks. However, the pick that selects to join your team may not be able to perform nearly as well as the first choice you just lost.

Male allies can create a culture of inclusion so when their organization gets the top draft-pick, top talent, regardless of gender, will want to play for their team, thus increasing their competitiveness. Some of the world's most influential institutions, including the Goldman Sachs, Ernst and

Young, the World Economic Forum, McKinsey, and others, have clearly demonstrated that women's full economic participation leads to greater competitiveness. Support from male colleagues supports the journey toward this greater competitiveness.

(Re)Building Your Network in an Expatriate Role

Proactively managing a network to reach career goals by winning support continues after making a career transition. The more significant the move, the greater risk of reducing the power and helpfulness of your existing professional network. In fact, many WiSER indicated that when moving to different organizations and countries, they temporarily lost their ability to perform at the same level because they no longer had the relationships they had cultivated over time, and they had to learn the local business subtleties. Professional networks are key to help you get your job done. When you know who to call and who to collaborate with, it will shrink your to do list more quickly and help you complete deliverables with greater ease.

As a female expatriate, tapping into professional networks in a foreign country may not be as simple as it seems. Potential complexities include language barriers and "old boys" network. As per WiSER Alexis, "At the start, particularly, you lose that network of working women that you've stored up over many, many years." She shared that "in a foreign country it takes a long while to build up [your network] because you don't have the school or university friends that you had before. I found the loss of the women's network the biggest thing to handle at the start." As she warns, often going to places like pubs with male colleagues in certain foreign countries can be misconstrued as something more than it is. Expatriate men can more readily build their professional network among other male expatriate colleagues and "old boys" networks. As per WiSER Alexis: "… there are certainly not many working expat women, and you can feel very lonely and you have to be very aware of that, and I think be strong enough to push through that."

It's a Wrap!

How many of you use your Google Maps or another GPS app to find your way around? Would you find your way if you didn't enter a destination? Knowing what you want from your career, and working with intention toward achieving those goals, is the essence of active career management. Building strong professional and personal networks, with people who can help you achieve your goals and those of the organization is crucial for a successful outcome. Such networks are comprised of mentors, sponsors, and allies who have targeted knowledge and know-how, to help you achieve your goals. Women are strong allies for women by being role models and showing them "how it's done." Men are strong allies as they are currently still the majority of decision makers and expatriates. As Jesse Owens once said, "We all have dreams, but in order to make dreams come into reality, it takes an awful lot of determination, dedication, self-discipline, and effort." Active career management can turn your dreams into reality.

CHAPTER 7

Operating Outside Your Comfort Zone

Security is mostly a superstition. Life is either a daring adventure or nothing.

—Helen Keller

International assignments exacerbate tensions that exist in any working woman's life because you are out of your comfort zone.

—Wiser Pauline

Your comfort zone is that sweet spot where you can perform well, with relative ease and without anxiety. When you operate within your comfort zone, your brain shifts into a kind of "automatic pilot" mode, and you perform your tasks without thinking too deeply about what you are actually doing. High levels of learning occur immediately outside of your comfort zone and can overwhelm far beyond your comfort zone (Figure 7.1). If you go abroad, where everything is likely to be new and different, you want to be prepared to move far beyond your comfort zone. WiSER Lindsay told us that even the smallest differences can make you feel a bit uncomfortable. "Prior to moving, I looked at the list of the team that worked for me," she said.

> I [thought to myself]: "G-E-R-G-E-L-Y Z-A-J-K-A-S? How on earth do I say that?" He likes to be called Greg, which is a lot easier, actually. But it was those kinds of strange things that make you feel really quite uncomfortable and unfamiliar.

As humans, we are creatures of habit and typically prefer some degree of certainty and predictability. Leaders, whether they are operating locally

Figure 7.1 Operating outside your comfort zone

or globally, must be prepared to deal with uncertainty. However, the level of uncertainty is bound to be especially high for expatriates where everything is new and different. Therefore, being able to operate outside of your comfort zone is crucial.

Operating outside your comfort zone may include taking risks, and it will require open mindedness and flexibility. "Be flexible," advised WiSER Martine.

> Don't try to continue doing things your way. Adjust to the culture that you are living in and remember you're a guest. That is very significant. What you do at home is your decision, but it is very important that you adjust to the world that you are living in when you are outside your own home.

She revealed how her own experiences in East Germany, in 1997, influenced her perspective on life. "In general, people are always complaining that we are going through so much change," she said. "When I moved to East Germany ... a few years after the wall came down, that's when I really realized how much change these people had gone through— and were able to cope with it." She noted that her colleagues in the former East Germany had witnessed more change than most people were likely to experience in a lifetime. "That is [a] very memorable experience that I've learned a lot from—also with respect to my own flexibility," she said.

Ultimately, working and living abroad stretches you beyond your current personal and professional boundaries. We defined the competency of "Operating Outside your Comfort Zone" as follows:

Operating outside your comfort zone
Embracing challenges coming from new experiences by tolerating ambiguity and remaining calm.
• You shift gears quickly and comfortably. • You learn quickly when facing a new problem. • You quickly grasp the essence and underlying structures. • You enjoy the challenge of unfamiliar tasks or situation. • You work constructively under stress. • You anticipate and manage effectively when facing unusual difficulties. • You have low security needs. • You deal constructively with own failures and mistakes.

Notably, 87 percent of the WiSER clearly demonstrated that they were able to operate, or were operating, outside of their comfort zone. All of those working on an international assignment in Africa and Asia were able to operate outside their comfort zone (100 percent), compared to 87 percent of those working in European countries and 75 percent of those working in North America. The percentage was lower (75 percent) among WiSER who had self-initiated their expatriation than among those women who had been sent abroad by their organization (91 percent).

On the spectrum of operating outside your comfort zone, where do you think you fall? Where would you like to be? What steps can you take to get there?

Routine ◀─────────────── **CHALLENGED** ───────────────▶ Panic

Our emotions range widely from positive to negative, with either extreme being unhealthy. When you are in the "Challenged" part of the Comfort Zone spectrum, this is where the greatest growth occurs. Undoubtedly, when you move abroad you may feel negative emotions more frequently because you are outside of your comfort zone and everything is foreign to you. You will encounter new situations, dilemmas, and emotions—and you may need to be creative in order to develop the right approach to address issues. The WiSER provided three best practices to manage stress, and build resilience, when you move outside of your comfort zone, in order to avoid moving into "Panic" on the spectrum and grow your professional capabilities.

Managing Stress

During an expatriate assignment, you must exercise global agility, push-ing yourself to "boldly go where no (wo)man has gone before." Diffi-culties are magnified, and you can no longer rely on your "automatic pilot." You may experience higher levels of uncertainty which can lead to panic, reacting rather than responding, poor decision making, poor health, and unhappiness. Instead, you must remain calm and focused. It is easy enough to speak of these things, but how does that work in practice? How can you manage anxiety and stress in order to concen-trate and perform well under such different, and in many cases difficult, circumstances? How do you avoid panicking? How do you make sure that the increased level of stress does not interfere with your power of judgment? How do you remain logical and not let your emotions get the best of you?

The human response to new situations is visceral. When we find ourselves in unexpected situations, for example when we experience the shock of a new culture, our limbic system is immediately stimu-lated. This means that our brain is struggling to determine whether this unexpected situation offers potential benefits or poses a significant danger. The more open-minded you are, the greater the chance that you will see the potential benefits of an unexpected offering. If you perceive an unexpected situation as dangerous, your mind moves to a "fight or flight" response, which essentially hijacks your higher rea-soning—the capacity for which you were hired. Severe stress can even morph strengths into liabilities that can derail the best of leaders. Let's illustrate this with a parable.

At a restaurant, a cockroach suddenly flew in through the window and sat on a woman. She started screaming out of fear. With a pan-ic-stricken face and trembling voice, she started jumping and swatting, with both her hands desperately trying to get rid of the cockroach. Her reaction was contagious, as everyone else in her group also got panicky. The woman finally managed to push the cockroach away but … it landed on a man from her group. Now, it was the turn of the other fellow in the group to continue the dramatic response. The waitress rushed forward to their rescue. In the chaos, the cockroach next fell upon the waitress. The waitress stood firm, composed herself and watched the cockroach on her shirt. When she was confident enough, she grabbed it with her fingers and threw it out of the restaurant. Was the cockroach responsible for the customer's hysterical behavior? If so, then why was the waitress not disturbed? She handled it without any chaos. It was not the cockroach that caused the chaos and the stress. Rather, it was the reaction to the cockroach. As an expatriate leader, outside of your comfort zone, it is important to remember that there will be many "cockroaches." It is even more important, to stay calm under stress and respond appropriately. The customers reacted, whereas the waitress responded. Reactions are instinctive, whereas responses are thought through.

As mentioned, when we are overwhelmed with new experiences, the "fight or flight" response will come into play, often resulting in flight. Recognizing this, WiSER advise you to "fight," in other words, step up to the challenge. WiSER Annette revealed in the interview that she forced herself to move beyond her comfort zone to explore a new city. "I was in Paris by myself for eight months, and I used to go home quite a bit over the weekends," she said. Recognizing that this was an opportunity to learn more about a major metropolitan center, she began to set aside time to explore the city. "One night a week, I would take the metro to somewhere that I'd never been to before," she recalled. "I would get something to eat in a restaurant, and then I would walk back to my hotel. Paris is really small, and I decided … I'm going to see Paris at least while I do this." The alternative, she realized was to spend time in a hotel room watching DVDs. "But what's the point?" she said. "You have to ask yourself, why are you are doing this? I think being able to be … tough on yourself is important." Following is a tool you can use to separate feelings from fact in order to identify and rationalize unreasonable emotions and manage stress (Table 7.1).

Additional stress management activities may include: eating and sleeping well; accepting that some things are outside of your control; remaining positive; developing greater emotional intelligence; practicing creative visualization; and venting your emotions by talking to a trusted confidant (such as a friend, a coach, or a counselor).

Table 7.1 Stress reduction exercise. Based on Laurel Mellin and University of California School of Medicine, Creating Effective Organizations

Stress reduction exercise—reviewing feelings vs. fact
Step One: Present the facts What are the facts and just the facts?

Step Two: Feel the feelings
 	
What are you feeling beyond the facts?
Identify feelings separately:
    1. I feel angry that…
    2. I feel sad that…
    3. I feel afraid that…
    4. I feel guilty that…
    5. I feel …

Step Three: Reason with the opposites
    1. Why am I feeling the emotions I have?
    2. What are reasonable/unreasonable thoughts?
    3. What would I like to feel?
    4. Challenge unreasonable thoughts and replace them with powerful, positive, and rational thoughts.

Step Four: Brain re-wire Repeat the powerful, positive, rational thoughts 10 times per day for 10 days

Step Five: Identify the actions
    1. What actions do I need to take in order to be effective with minimal stress?
    2. What support do I need, if any?

Building Resilience

Mental and physical resilience are essential if you want to be successful in an international role. "The most important thing is resilience," WiSER Annette contended. "You've got to be mentally and physically robust. It is tiring working in an unfamiliar environment [where] you have to be more on your toes. You have to be more prepared to deal with things that you don't know about." Moving abroad brings with it many changes, including tactical changes. Tactical changes in your daily life could involve (but aren't necessarily limited to) language, manners, food, communication style, public transportation, grocery shopping, schools, and access to technology. As WiSER Julie observed:

One of the best parts about living somewhere is actually, doing some of the mundane things, you know, like grocery shopping and dry cleaning and things like that to really get a sense of how a place works and how a culture works and to meet new people, that's really ... what it's all about.

Some of the things that we take for granted in our native country, however, may be less accessible in the host country, and when we have to take extra time to manage the tasks of everyday life, it requires a great deal of energy. When you start adding up those instances in which additional energy is required to deal with daily tasks, you start to get a feel for the kinds of pressures involved in an expatriate assignment. Now, factor in the tactical changes in your work environment. Among other things, you may encounter the following: local language in side conversations, different consensus-building styles, different teamwork styles, different decision-making processes, different leadership styles, unionized or non-unionized work environments, and a different legal and compliance framework.

To cultivate resilience, establish and practice small rituals that you can practice daily and maintain perspective. For example, Michael Phelps, a world-renowned swimmer, used to listen to music prior to a race so he could get in the zone. Although others tried to distract him when he was practicing his ritual, he remained steadfast and focused. Ideas shared by WiSER included rituals such as taking a one to two-minute break after 40 minutes of work; exercise; daily gratitude; and mindfulness.

Having a sense of humor is one good tool to maintain perspective. According to a study at Vanderbilt University, laughter burns about one calorie per minute; so, if you laugh 15 minutes a day, you can lose four pounds in one year. Laughter improves heart health, strengthens your immune system, and strengthens your abdomen. Take a moment to smile or laugh out loud. Those endorphins can reduce stress and help you to operate outside your comfort zone. "Take your work seriously but don't take yourself seriously," WiSER Sandra advised. You may find yourself in awkward cultural situations. In such situations WiSER Julie said: "Above all, maintain a sense of humor because a lot of times, it's the only thing that will get you through." As the humorous expression goes, "Don't sweat the petty things, and don't pet the sweaty things."

Building a Solid Foundation of Social Networks

Getting the foundation right is the most important part of constructing something new. The entire structure sits on top of the foundation. If there is a weak foundation, any mistake will only get worse as you go up, and if something fails, it's not easy to fix. The foundation of operating outside your comfort zone is the support of others around you and keeping a good sense of perspective. Social networks in your new venue will reduce loneliness and many of the discomforts of moving outside of your comfort zone. While you face a plethora of challenges during the adjustment period, mitigating loneliness will help shorten the transition period. Often the possibility to fall back on a social network (friends) will help you reduce the stress of expatriation as well. Therefore, taking immediate steps to build such relationships will lead to invaluable results. Things you can you begin doing to lay your foundation and create new social networks when expatriating may include:

- Attending or participating in events in your host community.
- Getting involved in boards, committees, or organizations where you can build relationships with other members of the expatriate community, while at the same time polishing your resume. Many of the WiSER are involved in groups such as the Girl Scouts, school boards, and non-profit organizations in their international venue.
- Building flexibility into your schedule. WiSER Joanne indicated that she arranged her work schedule so that she would be able to attend important school events.
- Seeking to build friendships among your colleagues. Some of the WiSER have shifted business meetings from a restaurant in order to invite their colleagues to dinner at their homes. You and your colleagues will get to know one another on a more personal basis, and this can be the beginning of establishing friendships among your co-workers.

- Scheduling activities you enjoy in order to meet like-minded people, whether these are dance classes, trips to the gym, running, biking, or cultural activities. These activities will bring you energy, enjoyment, and hopefully friendships.

It's a Wrap!

Operating outside your comfort zone involves having the ability to embrace challenges that derive from new experiences by tolerating ambiguity and remaining calm. Due to the high level of "new" and "different," international assignments tend to place additional demands on women to operate outside of their comfort zone. It may include taking risks and will require open mindedness. Ultimately, however, it involves stretching yourself far beyond your current personal and professional boundaries for the purpose of growth. While doing so, your comfort zone grows larger allowing you to manage stress effectively in order to improve work performance, while also maintaining your physical and mental health in an unfamiliar environment.

SECTION III

SECTION III

CHAPTER 8

The Culture Club

I don't want my house to be walled in on all sides and my windows to be stuffed. I want the cultures of all the lands to be blown about my house as freely as possible, but I refuse to be blown off my feet by any.

—*Mahatma Gandhi*

I didn't go in thinking I was going to change anybody; I just went in knowing that I was going to be changed.

—*WiSER Jacqueline*

How does culture impact success in an expatriate role? Culture influences the way that business is conducted, decisions are made, and how people interact with one another. Regardless of whether one selects to expatriate independently or through company channels, the level of role and responsibilities, or the type of organization, when working and living abroad, it is important to understand the cultural norms and values that are deeply rooted in a particular country. Greater understanding of a culture will positively affect how you engage with your colleagues, improve your level of acceptance and tolerance, and help you to operate in greater ambiguity in order to make solid decisions and recommend viable solutions that are feasible, timely, and acceptable. It is a common misnomer that many expatriates believe that they are brought in as experts and should have "all the answers." This misconception can often lead expatriates to believe that their knowledge is greater than that of the people who live there. WiSER Flavia advised expatriates against coming into a situation with an attitude of superiority. "They will just bear with you for as long as you have to be there, and just hope that the next time they'll be lucky and have someone else," she explained. "I think, going into any new situation with the curiosity to learn what they have to teach you—and not just with the pretension that you have things to teach them—is very important." In actuality, "the single most important element to establish a relationship with your hosts is to respect them," advised WiSER Flavia. "If they sense that you respect who they are and what they stand for, then you can do anything. I was extremely candid with my counterparts on matters that I thought needed to be addressed ..." She noted that she spoke frankly to employees about issues including inadequate skills, lack of commitment, and even corruption. "Yes, occasionally, you do get into a little bit of a tiff with some," she added. "But if you do it from the perspective that I really love this country, I really want to see it do well, that allows you to become a credible interlocutor who can—and is—legitimized to carry difficult messages."

The importance of cultural differences, when conducting business outside of our own nation, has been recognized for decades. L. Robert Kohls, an expert in the field of internationalism, describes culture as "an integrated system of learned behavior patterns that are characteristic of the members of any given society." For Kohls, the term culture encompasses "the total way of life of particular groups of people," including everything that group "thinks, says, does and makes." This culture is "learned and transmitted from generation to generation" (Kohls 1996, p. 23). In many ways, culture is like an iceberg, given that some parts a culture are visible to the naked eye, while others are hidden below the surface (Figure 8.1). WiSER Julie Anne admitted that it took her some time to discover those

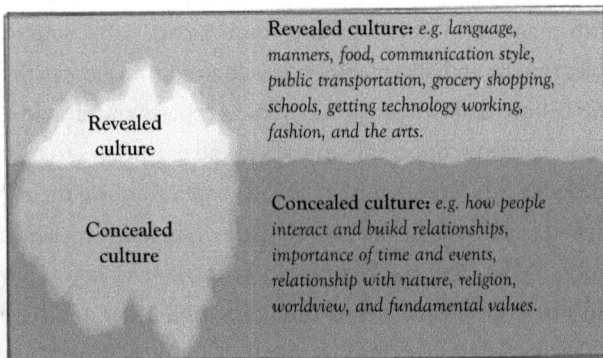

Revealed culture	**Revealed culture:** *e.g. language, manners, food, communication style, public transportation, grocery shopping, schools, getting technology working, fashion, and the arts.*
Concealed culture	**Concealed culture:** *e.g. how people interact and build relationships, importance of time and events, relationship with nature, religion, worldview, and fundamental values.*

Figure 8.1 The cultural iceberg

rules. She shared how tricky it was to understand concealed components of a culture, the hidden part of the iceberg.

> I got there and there were all sorts of unwritten cultural rules that were totally foreign to me. I had several examples of specific times when I thought, "how can I not figure that out?" But it took me probably a year or more into that assignment before I started to realize, "oh, that's what's happening." Then it became much easier for me.

The hidden, or "concealed," part of the culture is less accessible, but it is very important to understand. After all, it was the concealed portion of an iceberg that sunk the *Titanic*, and the concealed portion of a culture can "sink" you on your expatriate assignment.

Many cultural awareness courses and books written on the topic of expatriation focus on helping people who are entering new cultures to manage the "revealed" cultural aspects so that people can get on with daily life. Learning to look for external cues to see if we are doing the right thing is pivotal to managing revealed culture. In WiSER Emily's case, she found a need to adapt to local customs regarding attire. "I have made mistakes about clothing in places and that's not something I like," she acknowledged. "In Eastern Europe, it was [a] pretty sexist atmosphere, so I started dressing more conservatively." During an assignment in the Middle East, she had an embarrassing experience, when she wore a summer dress that turned out to be too short, by local standards. "Now, when I travel to the Middle East, I pretty much only wear pants," she noted. "I try to make sure that I prevent things that are going to make the fact that I am woman be an issue." WiSER, Diane, shared an example from her own experience. "In Asia, you are not likely to know that you've stepped wrongly," she said. "I mean, there [are] no clear signals. Now, you do that in West Africa, and they'll tell you. In Asia, you absolutely have to invest the time." Simply put, the tangible way to recognize cultural context is to consider timing, clues, body language, facial expressions (or lack thereof), intonation, and personal interaction. Consider the following situations, which demonstrate how "revealed" and "concealed" culture can affect a given situation. The subtleties are interesting, and they contribute to a complex tapestry that can be both challenging and enriching.

Situation #1: *Playboy Magazine*

Hans is from the Netherlands and works with a major global employer. He recently attended a global meeting in New York City, and while there, he and Jim, a colleague from the United States, got to know one another and built a positive working relationship. During the rapport-building process, Hans and Jim engaged in a casual conversation, and Jim shared the fact that he considered Bella Hadid to be extremely beautiful. Jim also told Hans that she was his favorite supermodel. A few months later, Bella Hadid appeared in *Playboy* magazine. Hans promptly picked up a copy of the magazine and, when he saw Jim at the next global meeting in the Netherlands, he presented the magazine as a fun gift. Well, it turned out that an American female colleague, who was in the room when Hans discretely handed over the magazine, happened to notice it and became very angry. She indicated that presenting a *Playboy* magazine to another man in her presence was offensive. Hans was perplexed. What would you do as the female colleague? Why was Hans confused? Was Hans right or wrong in his decision to give the magazine to his colleague? Download the Women Leaders Toolkit from the BEP Publishing website for additional tools and resources.

Situation #2: *Paint in the Amazon*

Carlotta secured a position with the United Nations immediately after earning her university degree. She was proud, and excited, to join one of the biggest NGOs in the world, whose mission was to "save the world" one action at a time. Shortly after she joined the UN, she was given a chance to join a team in Brazil. As it turned out, her first major assignment proved exceptionally challenging. Given that Carlotta was young and ambitious (and intent on a successful global career), she accepted the assignment without hesitation. She learned that there were three huge barrels of aluminum paint standing in a small village in the Amazon, and if the UN did not intervene, the villagers were going to dump the aluminum paint in the Amazon River, thereby endangering the local wildlife. The aluminum paint had been left in the village when the company that used it, lacked the resources to dispose of it properly. In the end, they abandoned the barrels in the village. Carlotta went to the village and assessed the situation, but she soon discovered she couldn't communicate with the villagers because they spoke in a tribal dialect. She recognized, however, that one young man was willing to help her, as he understood her and her purpose. The next morning, the young man came out, dressed in a Western suit and helped her organize a discussion around ways to remove the aluminum paint without dumping it in the river. He also helped to explain the ramifications of dumping the paint. She was grateful for his gesture, given that she felt the young man had helped her to meet her goals. She planned to thank him, yet, the next morning, the young man was nowhere to be found. Can you guess what happened to him? How was the mission accomplished? Download the Women Leaders Toolkit from the BEP Publishing website for additional tools and resources.

Notably, one complexity of concealed culture relates to gender relationships. Even in those countries where women occupy an increasing percentage of senior-level roles, gender issues remain prevalent. "You can't get upset by ... cultural issues," WiSER Anne stresses.

I remember, early on, if I shook the hand of a Muslim man, he would sometimes refuse to shake my hand, or he would cover his hand with a cloth to shake my hand, because women were impure. None of that ever bothered me. I never took it as insulting.

She treated these responses as a reflection of the individual's worldview, and while she didn't agree with his perspective, she didn't take these responses personally.

As Fons Trompenaars, a leading authority on cultural diversity in business, notes: "Every culture distinguishes itself from others by the specific solutions it chooses to certain problems" (2006, p. 8). These solutions are made on the basis of relationships with people as well as attitudes toward time and the environment. On occasion, our values and beliefs will conflict, and sometimes they will converge with the cultures we visit. Cultural differences are often a source of confusion, misunderstanding, and misinterpretation. If you have a clear understanding of these cultural differences, you stand a greater chance of working effectively with others in an international venue. Cultural experts have created various tools to assess and understand face value cultural differences. Download the Women Leaders Toolkit from the BEP Publishing website for additional tools and resources.

Seven Cultural Dimensions

One simple way to quickly identify some of the underlying values of any nation is to come up with a list of their common proverbs. These proverbs are a simple reflection of what is valued or promoted. A good example is, "God helps those who help themselves," a popular proverb in the United States that celebrates initiative. A common Dutch expression (translated into English) is, "adding water to the wine," which underscores a national tendency toward consensus building. Beyond proverbs, consider analogies, expressions, and jokes.

Language also tells you a great deal about the culture of a country. People appreciate it enormously when you attempt to speak the language, even if you are limited to a few words or polite expressions. Notably, language fluency positively impacts adjustment in the host country (Selmer 2015). All WiSER agreed that learning to speak the host country's language is very important. Yet, it is not always easy to learn a new language. What do you do then? How does that impact your working environment? WiSER Marjet, who works in Japan, shared some of her professional experiences. "I have a permanent translator who is my shadow," she revealed. "Everywhere I go, he goes, and that's the way it works." She admitted, however, that this situation is hardly ideal. "It's frustrating because you can never have a one-on-one with someone. You can never brainstorm. It's very difficult with the translator, and, of course, the limitation of the translator is also the limitation of the conversation." She noted that it becomes very difficult to discuss more complex topics such as the company's strategy, given that conversations usually remain at a basic level.

As we grow up among people who share the same norms and values, we expect them to behave in certain ways in certain circumstances. Although we are mentally prepared that people with different cultural backgrounds behave differently, emotionally we often find it difficult to accept these differences when we encounter them. We examine the world through our own cultural lens, and the greater the differences, the harder the adaptation (or settling process) is likely to be. We can distinguish seven dimensions where cultures differ. Five relate to the way people interact and how they build relationships, and two focus on how people interact with their environment (Table 8.1). These seven cultural

Table 8.1 Seven cultural dimensions. Adapted from Fons Trompenaars' cultural dimensions

Interaction with others	Beliefs and behavior	
Degree to which you do things by the book	Black and White: Rules are always applicable	Gray: Special circumstances and relationships may require exception to the rule
Degree of individualism	Part of a group	"Me, myself and I"
Degree of expressing emotion in interactions	Non-expressive	Expressive
Degree of importance of personal relationships for business purposes	Strictly business	Business is personal
Factors that are considered when judging someone's success	Achievement	Status
Relationship with environment	Beliefs and behavior	
The importance of time	Time	Event
The relationship with nature	Fatalistic	Own your destiny

dimensions, originally identified in 1997, continue to serve as a gold standard when it comes to understanding business across cultures (adapted from Trompenaars 1997).

The Degree to Which People Do Things by the Book

Does a rule always apply or are there exceptions to the rule due to special circumstances or relationships? Rigid application of the rules can sometimes give undesired results. Some cultures take that for granted, knowing that the consistent application of those rules create equality and certainty for all. In other cultures, it is acceptable to deviate from the rules to take special circumstances into consideration.

The Degree of Individualism

Do individuals see themselves as individuals or primarily as part of a group? Does the individual's interest come first, or is there a greater emphasis on the interests of the group? Many societies are deeply informed by collectivist values, a characteristic that WiSER Marjet encountered when working at a Japanese organization. "In Japan, they consult forever before they make a decision," she said. "That's part of the way they work and breathe and think." Although individual leadership is not altogether absent, there is a greater emphasis on consensus building. "They don't believe so much in leaders," WiSER Marjet explained. "You are part of the whole system (everyone is part of the whole system), and at the end of the day, of course, there is one top leader, but for that person just to express his or her opinion is …not the way it works."

The Degree to Which People Express Emotions in Interactions

How visibly do individuals show their feelings of anger, frustration, happiness and so forth? This difference proved a challenge for WiSER Marjet when she moved to Japan. She had a difficult time controlling the degree of emotion she expressed in a culture where emotional displays are culturally unacceptable. "I have a lot of expression in my face, a lot of nonverbal expression," she said. "That's something that's frowned upon in Japan. You should keep your thoughts to yourself, but I find it difficult to change that."

The Degree of Importance Placed on Personal Relationships for Business Purposes

Is doing business rational, transactional, "strictly business," or are personal relationships as much part of it, or maybe even a condition to do business and to work together? In some cultures, there is very little overlap between one's professional and personal life, as WiSER Lillian discovered when on an assignment in Germany. "Our work life and our personal life, with extremely few exceptions … don't mix," she said. "What we do at work is work; what we do at home is home, and there have only been just a couple of areas where that line has been crossed or blurred." WiSER Lillian indicated that she and her German colleagues often knew very little about one another. "When I came to Germany, I was actually quite surprised because I had two colleagues, who shared an office—and they had shared an office for over 10 years—and I asked one colleague, 'Does that person have children?'." The co-worker had no idea, she recalled.

"In Germany, there is more distance between work and personal [life], as compared to Italy or in Greece."

Meanwhile, WiSER Elsa I. discovered that there was a strong emphasis on personal relationships in Latin cultures. "I'd say that relationship is a big part of how work gets done there, and I probably underestimated how to leverage that," she said in the interview. She added that, if she had known what she currently knows, she would have approached her job very differently, and it would have helped her synchronize with the new organization much more quickly.

The Factors that are Considered When Judging Someone's Success

Are you considered to be successful and do you earn respect because of what you know and what you did (achievements), or because of who you know and who you are (status)? WiSER Alexis encountered unfamiliar attitudes toward authority when she accepted an assignment in the Czech Republic. "In Czech, I've had to adapt my style ... dramatically," she revealed. "I'm used to coming from an environment where I have to earn respect as the boss." This was not the case, however, when she assumed a position as CEO of an organization in Central Europe. "I'm automatically given enormous respect," she said. "They automatically think that I would know everything about what direction we should take, what decisions we should take, and they expected me to have a certain level of studiousness about me." In the end, these expectations led her to modify her management style. WiSER Alexis found that she needed to curb her sense of humor, because her employees expected their manager to be serious-minded.

Similarly, WiSER Anna found that traditional attitudes toward authority in Southeast Asia sometimes made it difficult for her to get honest feedback from her employees. "We tend to have a big Indian workforce and a big Filipino workforce, and they are extremely respectful to you," she said. "So, they are not going to tell you that you are wrong, or they're not going to tell you that's the best idea." The tendency of many workers to nod in agreement made it difficult to gauge their real attitudes. "People are not going to tell you automatically," she said. "You need to kind of figure it out yourself as well." However, the situation was very different in the UK, where employees challenged their managers on a regular basis.

"I think in the UK, one of the things I learned quite quickly is … stand your ground, but make sure you know what you're talking about," she said. "People respect you, if you know what you're talking about." WiSER Carrie discovered how status is attributed to age when she was working in South Korea. "The society is set up [with] … strict rules or norms … that you need to follow," she recalled. "For example, [with] a senior or junior man, the junior guy has to use a different language with this senior person." She noted that, in many situations, people are tacitly aware of who is the oldest, and this person will generally be treated with deference.

The Importance of Time

In some cultures, everything is driven by time, while in others, the event is of primary importance. WiSER Jacqueline noticed the differences during an assignment in Africa. "In Africa, there is [an] event culture, and I came from a time culture." She remembered when she and her husband had invited a group of people from four to six.

> [T]here is going to be a group that is going to leave at six, … but then there [will be] a group that's going to show up around 4.35 and they will stay until nine O'clock. The … getting together … was so much more important than the time.

While this required some adjustment, she found that she had to insist upon some degree of punctuality in the workplace. "I couldn't adjust to it too much in the workplace, so it was sometimes challenging with my staff to say, 'We need to be on time'. But I found in my own personal life [that] I made lots of adjustments." If you extrapolate the idea of time culture further, it defines a culture's sense of living in the past, present, or future. For example, Ireland is mired in folklore and their sense of present is strongly linked to their past identity. In the United States, a relatively young nation, people are very future focused.

The Relationship with Nature

Due to the somewhat abstract nature of this dimension, we will simply mention that it is the relationship people assign to their environment.

Some cultures live in harmony with nature, others control it, and others respect it at varying degrees. Further extrapolated and applied to business terms, this dimension influences whether people in a culture are more or less fatalistic or whether they feel they own their destiny.

Cultural dimensions are a logical series of categories to better understand revealed and concealed culture, which is key to supporting successful business interactions. Understanding your own cultural values and work style, and those of others will help you to work effectively in other cultures and decrease your ramp-up time to high performance. Once you understand the differences you can consider where and when to adapt.

To Adapt or Not to Adapt?

When we work and live abroad, we may assume that there is no tolerance for diverse approaches of thought and execution. We tend to believe that we should simply accept the way things are done there and "fit in." This can lead to "cognitive dissonance" between our internal values and the demands of an unfamiliar culture, which can create internal conflict and contribute to disengagement, poor performance, and a lack of personal fulfillment. Reducing levels of cognitive dissonance among expatriates can promote an easier adjustment, reduce stress levels, and decrease the chance of an early departure (Maertz, Hassan, and Magnusson 2008). As per WiSER Marjet,

> You want to hold on to your core beliefs and values. You need to be able to change colors without losing yourself, and that's the trick. If you lose yourself and become too much of a Japanese or too much of a Czech, you lose the strength that ... got you to that place and got you to that position in the first place. So, you have to find a balance there. That's actually adapting, but not changing.

To adapt or not to adapt, that is the question. You may embrace all, some, or no new habits from the host country. Each choice has its pros and cons (Figure 8.2).

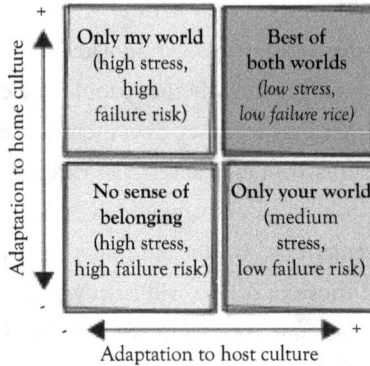

Figure 8.2 Model for cultural adaptation. Based on research by Maertz, Hassan, and Magnusson (2009)

"No Sense of Belonging"

Worst-case scenario. You no longer have a connection with your home country culture and values, but you have also failed to adapt to the host country. You don't feel you belong anywhere anymore. The result is high stress levels and a high risk of assignment failure.

"Only My World"

You do not adopt new cultural habits because you simply fail to understand them, or you don't want to adopt them, or you believe they conflict with your personal values. As WiSER Emily said:

> When something really doesn't feel right, it doesn't matter. You shouldn't have to accept it just because you are in an international environment. If it feels like supervisors are overstepping the lines of protocol between men and women, it doesn't matter that you are sitting in another country. You should be able to sort of step back and say, "That's unacceptable to me."

Failing to adopt any cultural habit of the host country, however, you remain an outsider, living in a country where you don't feel comfortable. The result is high stress levels and a high risk of assignment failure.

"Only Your World"

You adapt too well to the host country culture, and in doing so, you abandon your own values, and what you stand for. You risk "losing touch" with yourself if you become somebody else, if you become a "clone" of the locals. As WiSER Jacqueline cautioned:

> Don't try to become somebody (or something) else but learn from the culture and be willing to make some adaptations. You are never going to be a Kenyan [if you are not], but you can learn and grow and adapt to another cultural context ... I have seen too many extremes. I have seen lots of people who just go there and kind of throw off ... their own cultural heritage, and it just seems such a mistake.

The result is medium stress level, and a low risk of assignment failure.

"Best of Both Worlds"

This is the quadrant where you have achieved a balance between your host and home cultures. The new behaviors you adopt are considered up front, so you can stand behind your decision and feel comfortable about it. You adopt behaviors because you either like them, or you can live with them or justify them. At the same time, you may also choose to reject those host country behaviors that stand in opposition to your values. The result is low stress level, and a low risk of assignment failure.

In order to achieve peak performance in an expatriate role, it is key to adopt host country customs and behaviors that are in line with one's values. "I was very conscious of the fact that I had to learn the culture, tune in and learn and observe," recalled WiSER Hermie. "I was very conscious of that in my first couple of years because I was keen to be successful in my new environment." At either end of the spectrum, if you make too many concessions to the host culture or if you don't adapt at all, you will feel lost and alienated. As WiSER Martha put it: "When you live in multiple cultures, there are always pros and cons of every culture. So, you

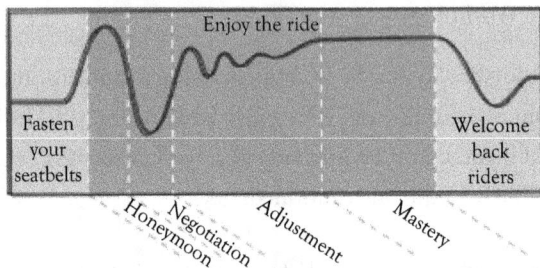

Figure 8.3 The emotional rollercoaster

have the opportunity to embrace what's wonderful about that culture. You can reject what you don't like."

Working and living abroad brings a roller-coaster of emotions, alternately feeling happy and then sad (Figure 8.3). This is called the expatriate cycle (Expat Explorer 2012). At first, everything seems new and exciting, and you find that there are many things to discover. This period is generally referred to as the "honeymoon phase." Within about three months, however, you will become sensitive to some of the differences between the host country and your home country, evidence that you have entered the "negotiation phase." Many of the differences you dislike become a source of annoyance and dissatisfaction, and in time, you may become homesick.

WiSER Andrea described her experience of the first two phases.

The first time that you move ... is the first time that you realize that you are basically on your own in a different country, that you don't have any kind of support system, that you have to build everything again from scratch, from zero,

she said. "In the beginning ... you are happy. Then, after this two to three-month period ... comes the homesick time, when you start to compare everything, and you miss everyone, and you miss everything in your daily life." It will take another few months to find yourself in the "adjustment phase." At this point, the host country starts to feel less foreign, and you feel more confident. You become familiar with the different routines and customs and start to understand the new culture and to accept the differences. In the end, you will feel comfortable in the new country. You will find your place in the local community and identify ways to combine the new culture with your own.

It's a Wrap!

Cultural norms are the underlying reasons for different behaviors including how people interact and build relationships. Some of the differences will be obvious, but many cultural norms and values will be concealed and difficult to recognize. There are seven different cultural dimensions, of which five influence interpersonal relationships: the degree to which a culture places group interest vs. individual interest; the degree to which people of a culture express emotions; the degree to which a culture values building a personal relationship prior to engaging in business activity; and the degree to which success is measured based on personal achievement or status. Each culture also has a unique relationship with time and environment. When combined, these dimensions highly impact how people interact, and business gets done. When adapting to a new culture, find the right balance between adopting new behaviors and staying true to yourself. Understanding the way you work with others, combined with understanding how other cultures work, equals success.

CHAPTER 9

Your Debut

You never get a second chance to make a good first impression.
—Will Rogers

I didn't want to like her, but I ended up liking her. She is fantastic.
—Male colleague of WiSER Alicia

When the time comes for a woman to make her debut in an expatriate role, it is important to operate from a position of personal power where she recognizes that she was the one selected among many other talented professionals because her talents can help the organization meet its goals. Due to the incredibly high standards women often hold themselves to, they, more so than men, tend to question their abilities and use luck as a reason for their success, despite their competence. As women consider their initial entrance to a new job, work team, nation or culture, they will be forced to fundamentally rediscover themselves. Their debut will leave critics reeling only if they can operate at an optimal level quickly. An analysis of all CEO transitions in Fortune 500 companies over a 15-year period found that women were more likely than white men to be promoted to CEO of firms who had been performing poorly for some time. This means that it fell upon them to improve results under very difficult circumstances. This also means they were at fault if things didn't improve drastically. With female leaders often being under close scrutiny, accelerated ramp up time to peak performance is of the essence (Dishman 2018).

The majority of the WiSER we interviewed indicated that the first 90 days of an expatriate role were the most challenging—and the most critical for success. Positive first impressions in the first 90 days are essential to be impactful and be recognized for contributions. Yet, this a period where "leaders trip on pebbles." During a recent conversation with Bob, Talent executive, he noted that leaders, especially global leaders, have generally found themselves in that position because they are proven entities. They have shown that they possess the knowledge, skills, and abilities to fulfill their roles. If that's the case, why do these leaders sometimes fail?

They don't fail because they've tripped over a boulder; they fail because they've tripped over pebbles.

Regardless of what you trip over, there is a pursuant fall. Women expatriates will encounter even more "pebbles" due to the bell curve. The first 90 days is an interesting period of balancing what is new and interesting with the unfamiliarity of the new role and the dynamics of a new team. During this period, colleagues are looking for the answers to several questions. Are you competent? Are you trustworthy? Are you someone to approach or avoid? Do you have status and authority? Are you simply interested in upgrading your resume, or are you vested in the team's success? "It is crucial to earn trust and credibility in your environment, particularly in an international environment," WiSER Hermie stressed.

The first 90 days are an opportune time to win the respect of local and expatriate colleagues by demonstrating that you are skilled and competent. Identify viable opportunities for early "wins" that will help you to establish your credibility with your new management, colleagues, and staff. "I think the competency in your field becomes more critical because it helps people overcome any particular assumptions they may make of you because of a cultural background or the fact that you're an American, or whatever," WiSER Pauline stated.

As soon as you show your competency in the given field, people stop talking. I mean, at the end of the day, people are rewarded for performance. People are respected for the results they deliver, and if you deliver, most people will park any other questions.

Making the Move

Notably, the initial period of taking a new role is a vulnerable time that is fraught with challenges. In expatriate roles, there is a greater likelihood of encountering "pebbles" than "boulders" given the complexities of a new culture. "Surviving the first few months of being abroad, being away from your family, from friends, that's difficult because it's very challenging," WiSER Argentina observed. "We don't know our surroundings, and then, the language is different. The habits are different." To make matters worse, she found herself alone and isolated on most weekends. "I cried many times in those days," she said. "I think that my boss kept saying: 'No, no, no, it's okay. It's normal.'" At some point, when her boss found her particularly upset, she said: "Well, if you are about to cry, I have many things to cry about, we can both cry. But if you want, we can also have fun. We can go out—and I was coming here to invite you to come out." The exchange ended in laughter, and those kinds of supportive friends helped her get through the first few months of her assignment. While you face a plethora of challenges during the adjustment period, bear in mind that what you stand to gain from an international assignment far outweighs the challenges and hardships you may feel intensely upon your arrival.

When moving to another country, the change that will be experienced can be framed in two dimensions. At a practical level, during your daily routine, you will experience "country shock"—adjusting to a new physical environment and "culture shock"—adjusting to new people and practices. To compound matters, this all happens during a period when you are making your first impression in a new job.

Country Shock

When moving abroad, there are many new things to get used to—a new climate, new faces, and a new currency—just to name a few. In addition, you are doing without many of the things to which you were accustomed to at home. If relocating to a developing country, there are even more challenges to face, including poor communication/technology infrastructure, frequent electricity fall-out, fuel shortages, and substandard roads. The physical environment in which you will operate is entirely different from what you are used to. Transportation, communication, and daily life are less fluent and timelines to complete a task or achieve goals will be longer than planned for. Adapting to a new environment will involve setting up new routines which requires thinking continually about the simplest tasks in life, therefore, draining energy normally reserved for "sophisticated" tasks. WiSER Pauline explained that you will usually have to factor in more time and planning for simple tasks. "You're not on your home turf," she said. On more than a few occasions, you will feel incompetent and frustrated. WiSER Emily shared a humorous story involving her own efforts to adapt to a new environment. "I remember when I moved to Hungary," she said.

> Hungarian is a completely different language, and so there is just no way of understanding until you learn it. I think I had been there about a month and everything was going fine, but I had this whole nervous breakdown one night because I accidentally bought ... what I thought was laundry detergent.

In the absence of a washing machine or Laundromat, she had adopted the habit of washing her clothes in the sink, and she was shocked at the results when she poured the contents of the bottle on her clothes. "I threw all this bleach ... onto my jeans, and I only brought ... two suitcases with me," she recalled. "They were covered with these white streaks, and I ended up sobbing, and my roommate thought, 'Why is she sobbing over some jeans?'" Her response to the incident, of course, was a reflection over her larger frustration with the language barrier. Overall, our advice is to maintain perspective. It will get better!

Apart from the need to reestablish daily routines, the demands of a new job will require a good deal of time and energy. Hence, the first months in a new host country are likely to be exhausting. WiSER Joanne revealed that her biggest move was actually her first one. She had been with her organization for almost 20 years when she was recruited for a leadership position. "It was a very emotional and personal change in my life, and that of my family," she recalled. "But in hindsight, it was only nine days. Once, you make that big move, the rest of the moves become easy."

Culture Shock

Culture shock is brought on by stress resulting from losing cultural clues—the signs and symbols that guide social interaction. These clues, which may be words, gestures, facial expressions, customs, or norms are acquired by all of us in the course of growing up and are as much a part of our culture, as the language we speak or the beliefs we accept. When an individual enters a strange culture, all or most of these familiar cues are removed. He or she is like a fish out of water (Oberg 2012).

Adjustment to a new country is often complicated by the fact that that people tend to glorify certain aspects of their home country and view many aspects of the new country in a negative light. WiSER Erica observed that romanticizing the past limits your capacity to work with the people who are right in front of you. "Throughout my career I have heard a lot of people talk and reminisce about the past. They say things like 'Oh, when we had this, when we had that, we used to do it this way,' and so on. This is the worst thing to do," she noted. "This new country and this new group of people that you work with accepted you with open arms, and you need to be respectful and be positive ... don't compare."

Making an effort to integrate into your new community will help reduce culture shock and get you settled in more quickly. The WiSER engaged in activities such as participating in sports, taking language courses, going out socially with colleagues, and so on. Even though an expatriate role if often temporary, the key to integrating it to treat it as if it was the rest of your life. Making decisions and building relationships with a long-term view is beneficial. Whereas, decisions based on the perception that an assignment is temporary could include failing to join clubs and other social organizations and neglecting to reach out to neighbors. WiSER Andrea concurred.

> For me, every time I go, I always think I could be here forever. So, I [might] as well ... get engaged in things, understand the local politics, learn the language, mix with the people—and that is something that makes you learn much more and enjoy much more than if you are just thinking of that as an assignment.

It should be noted, however, that efforts to engage in some countries as a single woman can be challenging. WiSER Claudia described an experience she had in Panama. "Prostitution is not a crime here, so there are a lot of prostitutes. So, going out at night was a problem ... I could not go to a bar on a Friday night to make friends, because here it's impossible to do because of this cultural aspect." So, she concentrated on out-of-work activities that involved safe environments. "In the first week, I found out where I could go for dance classes, swimming classes, and I started having like three kinds of activities outside work," she recalled. "Maybe if I were a guy, I could just go to a bar and make friends," she conceded. "Yes, it would be easier." Again, adjusting is not always easy, but engaging in activities that give you energy and put you in contact with like-minded people will make you feel at home before you realize it.

There are signs and symptoms that that can help you recognize when you or a loved one is experiencing country or culture shock (Table 9.1). One of the WiSER told us that she was expecting to come home one day and see her husband and children on the couch, in a dark room, with arms crossed, saying that they were miserable and wanted to go home. Luckily for her this never happened. The key is to understand that country and culture shock are temporary conditions—not only for you, but also for your family. You will need to assist your family members during their adaptation period. "You are going to have an increased accountability to your family ... [something] you don't feel in your home country, because your spouse and your kids are more independent in their home environment," WiSER Elsa I. advised. "You put them out of that [environment],

Table 9.1 *Overall signs and symptoms of culture and country shock*

Emotional signs	Symptoms
Sadness/depression	Headaches, pains, and allergies
Anger	Over-concern about your health
Vulnerability	Insomnia or sleeping too much
Irritability	Obsessed with cleanliness
Loneliness	Withdrawal
Shy/insecure	Idealizing you own culture
Homesickness	Trying too hard to fit in
Lost/confused	Smallest problems seem overwhelming
Boredom	Questioning your decision to move to this place
Frustration	Stereotyping of host nationals
Anxiety	Hostility toward host nationals

and now you have—at least in my mind—an accountability to minimize the isolation they might feel or smooth the transition for them."

Avoid the Pebbles

Strategically navigating the political landscape, leveraging networks combined with effective cross-cultural communication will enable you to avoid the pebbles and make a star-studded debut.

Influence Through Networks

Professional networks, formal or informal, are foundational to success in your new role. They are an optimal means to learn what is going on, enhance organizational influence, and adapt more quickly to your new environment. Although each person that moves to another country has to build a new network within the organization, women expatriates are significantly better at coping with that initial isolation. Women are used to operating as a minority in an environment where the majority of power is held by men. Therefore, they have learned to attain their goals through influence and collaboration. While climbing career ladders, many women are accustomed to being a minority, especially in leadership positions, and therefore, they are used to being excluded from existing networks. As women work to identify and cultivate new professional networks, it is important to identify multipliers and stakeholders who can help navigate the political landscape in the new organization.

In the world of organizational transformation, there is a mantra "culture eats strategy for breakfast." Organizational culture is the pulse of an organization drives what is politically suitable, feasible, and acceptable. WiSER Gillian recommended to learn as much as possible about the new landscape. "Culturally and politically, I had to learn how to work differently," she recalled. "I had to understand where the key sensitivities were, and who the key stakeholders were." She added: "So, I had to learn to work with the politics … check out and try to find out what the rituals are at work, what things are said, how they are said, and find out who the key players are." Establish connections with your new workplace and colleagues and get a clearer understanding of expectations and goals for the position.

Leveraging influential networks to achieve goals that benefit the organization or individuals within is how work gets done. It is critical to understand team dynamics, the political environment, and various competing agendas. "You have to understand the dynamics in teams, in power, in authority, so that you understand how you can be effective and address issues while being respectful … of the way things are," WiSER Diane observed. First, decide on a goal. Have you been hired to change the organizational culture, to launch new initiatives, to bring in certain skills and expertise, to reorganize the organization and fire people, or perhaps to fill a managerial skills gap? WiSER Nathalie K. offered advice based on her own experience. "I think it's important to understand…[what] your role is, and what is expected of you within the organization," she explained. "And that may evolve as you are there, but it provides clarity not just for yourself, but for the people around you on what they can expect from you as well." Second, anticipate who will support or resist your agenda, and determine whose support is needed to move your agenda forward. Leaders who are politically competent understand that they need the support of others to succeed. They appreciate when and when not to act. They anticipate how people may react to their idea, what their motivations are and identify variables that may influence people when their idea is introduced, or the meeting plays out. They find out what their goals are and determine how they align (or not) with their own goal. It allows them to prepare options and a plan, so they can react quickly in a fast moving, potentially political environment. Third, rally support to help you achieve your goal by communicating benefits and building coalitions that will support the goals you strive for. There is no such thing as a "self-made" (wo)man. Let the stakeholders know that you are working on their behalf and engage them to invest in your success. Align your agenda to theirs. It is important to depersonalize the political situation even if your goal is not met. This is easily said and not easily done. By bearing in mind that another goal being moved ahead is not a personal attack, there is a better chance to objectively contribute to the goal agreed to and live to champion your goal(s) another day.

Stay plugged in to your office and office politics if you want to get the things done that need to be done in your organization and make a positive impact in your first 90 days. Women are often so busy working, that they isolate themselves. They focus on the client or customer to the point that they may forget to build internal alliances and networks. Women should line up a coalition of supporters—allies, advocates, mentors, and sponsors—in order to garner support to achieve goals. Such a strategic network will be willing to expend political capital on your behalf. The fact is, one of the most effective ways to achieve your targets is to focus on the people you will need to make it happen. WiSER Diane shares, "You have to recognize that it's people who are going to achieve that," she said. "As I always say to people, between you and the outcome that you are trying to achieve … is a person. So, you need to focus on the person that's in front of you."

Having a sense of connection has been shown to positively impact productivity and emotional well-being. From an evolutionary perspective, sticking together improved our chances of survival. An effective leader contributes to a positive culture, engaging people with different talents from various departments to create solutions and achieve results. WiSER Martha: "People can sense when you're genuine, when you really care, when you really want to make a difference. … I always want to bring out the best in people and think that helps to draw teams together. As a leader, the mindset of 'I need you and the perspectives and the skills that you bring' helps to create teams that can deliver."

Influence Through Communication

Effective communication is an important tool to positively impact your first impression. Communication encompasses the way you present yourself, and the manner in which you express your ideas. Your ability to effectively communicate will be the basis upon which your new colleagues will develop an opinion about you. Cultivate strategic communication capabilities in order to influence others' perception of your capabilities and improve recognition and reward.

Often women are avid communicators, yet not perceived as strategic. Research has shown that managers rated women higher than men in leadership competencies, but lower in leadership potential (Zenger 2012). We all have the opportunity to impact others' perception of us through effective and confident communication. However, research also shows that women have a greater challenge owning success, demanding recognition and projecting confidence. In order to be a strategic communicator, it is critical to create impact through a concise approach, powerful language, and solid questions. In other words, come prepared and overcome the "common information effect." In layman's terms, the "common information effect" is essentially groupthink that occurs when there is a lack of trust and lack of diversity of thought. Women often speak when they are in agreement. In order to be strategic, women have a responsibility to get a fresh idea, their idea, in the conversation first. Vetting ideas in advance is another empowering way to get your voice in the room. Voicing opinions is a positive component of effective communication to garner equity. High stakes situations require that one engages in strategic conversations. To do so, it is imperative to clearly describe the situation and its impact on you, the client, the company. Prepare a few ideas regarding the situation and your desired solution or view. It is important to stand your ground and always end with agreement, even if you agree to disagree.

Communication is, to a great extent, shaped by cultural norms, and it is imperative to modify or adapt your communication styles in order to be understood (and to avoid being misunderstood) when working in different countries. "I absolutely modify my communication style depending upon the cultural context I am working in," noted WiSER Sandra. Communicating effectively in an international environment requires a mastery of a range of skills, including speaking, presenting, writing, and listening. In addition, you need to "read" the unspoken in various settings, ranging from one-on-one encounters to presentations before large audiences. Here is a list of five recommendations to effectively communicate across cultures that were shared by the WiSER.

Follow Cultural Protocol

When communicating through any medium, considering cultural protocol and preferences will improve effectiveness. The directness and formality of language varies from culture to culture. Whether they use titles, operate on a first-name basis, write or speak casually or formally is directly informed by cultural norms. In the United States, for example, you are likely to be on a first name basis with all your colleagues, including your superiors. In Germany, relationships are much more formal, requiring you to formally address not only your superiors, but also your peers, your secretary, and even persons who are younger than you are, for example, Mr. Zimmermann or Frau Dr. Decker-Conradi. Following is an example of how directness differs from culture to culture. WiSER Maria encountered this challenge when working in Canada. "Canadians avoid confrontation—let's say it like that," she noted. "Whenever they have to give a tough message, they give it in a very non-confrontational way." She observed that people in her native Belgium, on the other hand, tend to be far more direct. "It's not that we are impolite," she explained. "[It's] that we just give the messages in a more direct way, and when I speak English, or when I translate my Dutch to the English, I would be quite direct." While her style of communication discomfited many of her Canadian colleagues, none of them raised the issue in a conversation. "Nobody would ever tell me ... I wasn't aware of that until I got that feedback on paper," she recalled. "Then, I realized that I had to adapt my communication style."

WiSER Martha observed that in spoken communication, this includes the manner in which you interact with superiors, and the way you greet people or initiate a conversation. It is also important to consider the company culture, which is often reflected in lingo and colloquialisms. We recommend that you familiarize yourself with company language and that it is used sparingly in order to keep things simple and clear. WiSER Annette explained that modes of explanation that are effective in one culture may not work as well in another. "One thing I have learned is that [some] cultures like storytelling," she explained. "And by that I mean, when you are trying to ... give an example ... you say, 'I think you should do "X", and this reminds me of a project ... where we were looking at "Y," and we decided to do "A-B-C," and this turned out to be a good decision.'" She noted that this kind of storytelling worked well in the Middle East, where people preferred concrete examples that were based on personal experience. However, these long, personalized explanations tended to bore German workers, who were inclined to request that she get to the point and provide concise directions.

When preparing written communication in an international environment, bear in mind that the communication may be received or delivered by non-native English speakers. WiSER Julie Anne said. "People may not understand your point when you're giving a speech, but if you are following it up with something in writing that's well written, they'll get it, even if it's not in their native language." Similarly, WiSER Emily stressed the need to write in a straightforward manner, given that you will often address people with an imperfect grasp of English. Notably, consider writing protocols in the host country. "When you write an e-mail to an American, and you put exclamation marks at the end of a sentence, that typically means that you are yelling at them. In Germany, it means important," WiSER Magi explained. She recalled that she took time to explain the difference to both her German and American colleagues because it had given rise to irritation and misunderstandings.

Ask Questions

Asking questions is among the quickest ways to harness the knowledge of others, and to gain an understanding of your new environment. This element of leadership is more important than ever in an international environment. Rather than arriving on the scene with all the answers or taking a one-size-fits-all approach, harness the skills, talents, and ideas of new teams and organizations. This approach demonstrates an interest in learning about the team and the unfamiliar customs, norms, and values of the host country. "I wasn't afraid to ask questions," WiSER Magi recalled. "There was this particular person that my husband worked with—whom we got along with very well—, and I said: 'You know what? I am having a hard time with this.'" She went on to discuss with him some of her challenges and asked for his feedback on the appropriate response. "And I would be open to talking to [him] about things like that because he knew his people," she explained. "He knew the culture, he knew the industry, and he knew what would be okay or not okay for me to say ... It just helps that you are able to ask the questions, because if [you] don't ask, you are never going to know." Magi shared her uncertainties with an outside confidant. However, you can find plenty of people to approach within your organization as well.

Asking questions improves opportunities to get honest feedback and enhance team collaboration. It is not always easy to determine what the right questions are, but, if at first you fail, try again. WiSER Stacy indicated that she would occasionally throw out an idea and gauge the reception. At one point, she observed that everyone had been working hard and suggested that it might be a good idea to grant some "comp-time" as a reward. "Everyone said: 'Yes, yes. Great idea,'" she recalled. Before the roll out, she asked a variety of questions. She asked about issues including time accrued and whether time off would be valued and looked upon as a reward. It was only when asking these questions that Stacy learned that many workers had so much time left, that they didn't need extra compensation time and wouldn't use it anyway, if they felt like they had to get their work done. WiSER Sezin indicated that, in certain cultures, subordinates will not correct a supervisor if not explicitly asked to do so. In one case, she sent out a letter that included inaccurate information that her team had failed to point out. "The team … came back to me, screaming, saying 'How dare you do that?'" Sezin was stunned and told them that she thought they had agreed the content of the letter was correct. "If there was an inaccuracy, why didn't you tell me?" she asked them. They told her that they didn't say anything because she was the boss, and she should know. "So, since then, I actually drill and drill and drill and drill until I get to the bottom of things," she said.

Practice Active Listening

Listening and observing are the "better half" of good communication. As the saying goes, God gave us two ears and one mouth because listening is twice as important, but twice as difficult. In an international environment—where there are different levels of knowledge of the language, different communication styles, accents, and body language—listening and observing skills are even more important. "I don't think listening is an inherent talent that a lot of us have," WiSER Pauline said. "But I think listening becomes even more important when you're working in a multicultural environment." To be an effective listener involves listening without thinking about what you will say next—and remaining focused. It means to acknowledge the person you are listening to. It is best to save judgments for later, after you have heard and understood what was said.

Active listening leads to increased receptivity to the unspoken. Read between the lines, look for hidden messages and become adept at "reading" body language. Hearing what is *not* being said can serve as a valuable road map to understanding people in a country other than your own. It can also help you avoid miscommunications. Women's generally acknowledged strong sensitivity to non-verbal signs, enables them to learn faster and establish relationships in the host country, which serves as an advantage when expatriating (Haslberger 2007). "You have to have the ability to pick up on signals, to read between the lines, because the cues are certainly not what you're used to," WiSER Pauline explained. "The hidden messages are not what you grew up with. It's much, much more complex when you're working in an international environment."

WiSER Jolanda agrees that unspoken messages are often the most important. "If you get an e-mail or letter from somebody from the UK, and it's more than four or five sentences long, it means there's something wrong because they're like the Japanese. They cannot say, 'no,'" she explained. "If they become long and windy, it means you're actually hitting them somewhere where they feel very uncomfortable, and they actually want to say to you, 'Don't do that.' But it doesn't really say that in that e-mail." In addition to reading unspoken cues of others, find quiet moments to pay attention to what you are "hearing" from your own body and what unspoken signals you are emitting. Manage your body language and signals with intention.

Be Clear

Communicating with clarity is often more challenging in a different cultural setting. It may require more discussion, slower delivery, leveraging visuals, or even using hand signals—especially in cases where you speak the local language poorly, or few of your colleagues have a strong grasp of your language. It is never a mistake to repeat things in such situations, and it is better to take the risk of over-communicating rather than to under-communicate. "I am very conscious of making sure I try to explain myself so that people aren't misreading my actions because of their own personal cultural context," WiSER Sandra explained.

I had to learn to be more direct. While superficially, my international team seemed to have good English skills, they could speak better than they could understand. It was a real challenge in terms of actually learning to be very precise with words.

Sandra had to learn to communicate in a manner that was concise and direct, despite the fact that this style of communication would have been considered rude in her native UK. When language fails, resort to visuals, suggested WiSER Carrie. "I drew a lot of pictures and I used a lot of hand signals," she said. "I always had a whiteboard in my office, because you sometimes need to show people up or down or across or boxes or charts or something visual."

Communicate Respectfully

As bright as you may be, and as much as you have learned about your business, your industry, and your organization, you are going to have to relearn some of those lessons with a different set of eyes, given that cultural differences are very real. "Definitely don't judge in your first year," WiSER Britta advised. As WiSER Veronika shared:

Never judge people because of how they present something, how they actually talk over the phone, never judge anybody's competence or skills just due to this factor … Some very good technical people … just don't come across as good because they are not very good … in English. But it has nothing to do with that you are not good or bad, it's more about communication.

Humor differs among countries and can be interpreted as disrespectful, impolite, and insincere. Also, sarcasm which is typically a cutting remark that takes the form of humor, does not translate with respect in many countries. It is not an element of effective communication in domestic settings, and it can be destructive in an international environment.

Showtime!

Making an impressive international debut, will require maintaining an open mindset and taking impactful actions in the first 90 days. At this point, women will need more than just a script … it's time to take stock of all the supplies, costumes, props—the full arsenal. There are real barriers stopping women from moving into leadership roles—the glass ceiling—as well as into international roles—the glass border. However, there are also real opportunities to dismantle those barriers. In order to be on stage, it is important to remember that a stellar performance was and will continue to be imperative. Your technical skills may help you get the job done, but leveraging your global leadership competencies, will allow you to get the job done well. Due to the unique position female expatriates are in, developing and mastering the four WiSER competencies—self-awareness, conscious imbalance, operating outside your comfort zone, and active career management—will lead to a great showtime.

Self-awareness will be your compass as you consider how to adapt, while staying true to your values, and help make critical decisions. The first 90 days is usually the most difficult period in an international assignment. Therefore, it is a time when the scales will be consciously imbalanced and tipped severely toward work during the initial period of an expatriate role. "The first month, you are on the go 24/7, whether it's work or getting yourself and your family settled," WiSER Joanne warned. It is a good time to review and re-calibrate the scales after the first 90 days.

As you make your debut, identify what you want from this opportunity, and build networks to help you achieve your goal. Building professional relationships with superiors, peers, teams, and clients quickly is essential to make good business decisions and get some "wins" early on. In order to build robust networks, bear in mind that it is a two-way street. WiSER Elsa who was the first female Head of School in a South American country: "I think my philosophy … is that you really have to focus on making the people around you be as successful as possible … give them as many opportunities as possible and make them as successful as they can be." This network is also foundational to navigate the international landscape and grasp its subtleties and nuances.

When you combine relocation with starting a new job, and then add pre-existing notions or stereotypes about your nationality and/or gender, you can easily find yourself in an explosive situation. Therefore, you need to be prepared to stretch yourself in ways that may strike you as unprecedented, and you will have little, if any, downtime. WiSER Erica advised.

"Stay positive, because [it's the time] when you learn about the new company, meet new people, learn new ways of doing things … it is probably one of the most stressful things you will do, so it is imperative that you focus on integrating and settling [yourself and] your family as quickly as possible." She added, "If they are happy, you will also be happy—and successful." During this remarkably stressful period, we recommend that you immediately identify one, two, or three healthy habits that you enjoy and will engage in regularly in order to better manage stress. These are habits that will bring discipline into your life, and it is essential that you be able to engage in these habits without having to rely on anyone else. "I always kept reminding myself of what I wanted to be or to achieve," WiSER Argentina noted. "Also, I use three things that really help me stay focused. I exercise between two to four times per week. I pray. I read a lot. I enjoy reading books that will teach me something."

Remember to learn about the host country to understand what makes them tick. Develop your own opinions regarding your host country and new job based on objective information. WiSER Lindsay advised, "Work-wise, you have to be quite culturally open-minded, and not have negative biases or perceptions about people or stereotypes." If you have a partner and/or family, you are not the only one who will live and operate in the new culture. They will experience the differences as much as you will, and therefore, it is advisable to take steps to prepare them too. Take care of those with you, and they will take care of you.

Now that you have made your debut as a female expatriate, let's assume the critics are raving about your performance. How can you use the stellar performance review to land the next role? Share successes by keeping lines of communication to decision makers open. As WiSER Pauline told us: "The advice I would give is to keep a connection back to your home organization" she said.

> That is absolutely critical. You've got to keep your network up. You need to keep in touch with what's going on back home because the risk is that you can indeed be forgotten about. You're out of sight, out of mind as they say. Depending on what kind of talent management your company has, it is really important to keep that connection back to your base.

Working and living abroad is the most powerful development tool. Leveraging this experience to accelerate your professional trajectory starts by making sure it will be a visible feather in the cap. If you set out to define yourself as a leader of tomorrow, expatriate roles, both short and long, can serve as a fast track. As the need for talented leaders is concerning CEOs around the world, expatriating to accelerate development is a solution to increase the percentage of women in leadership pipelines. For women reading this book, if you want to define yourself as a leader of tomorrow, there is no better time for you to expatriate and fast-track your professional and personal growth.

It's a Wrap!

In an expatriate assignment, your first 90 days will be filled with a series of (thirty-seconds) first impressions, so you need to make them count, even under challenging circumstances. Immediately after international relocation, there are two categories of shock to the system. Country shock and culture shock can lead to stress caused by operating in a new and unfamiliar environment and stress from losing cultural clues used to guide social interactions. While facing these stressors, you are concurrently entering a new role in a new country and have to make a positive debut. Rather than look for boulders blocking your path to success, it is key to identify pebbles you may trip over. The best way to maneuver a new expatriate role is to influence through professional networks and effective cross-cultural communication. When relocating, there is a loss of a professional network which can result in a struggle to get the job done expediently, keep abreast of current happenings, and exert influence through key stakeholders. Therefore, it is very important to establish your new network of "go to" people through intentional relationship building and strategic communication efforts to foster a smooth transition. Strategic communication improves effectiveness and facilitates a smoother transition. Stay positive and focus on cultivating global leadership and WiSER competencies to achieve peak performance at an accelerated rate.

APPENDIX A

Gender Parity Spotlight™ Survey Details

For a full copy of the report please go to https://leveragehr.com/in-the-press

Research Details

The questions of the survey, held in November 2017, were based on the Gender Parity Spotlight™ (GPS) survey which was created to obtain a baseline of data to create a targeted strategy to retain and grow the women in their specific organization. The GPS is based on extensive research conducted by Leverage HR to find out what types of barriers prevent women from accepting or gaining leadership positions in organizations. Specifically, Leverage HR reviewed the published literature, conducted over 60 interviews of female executives, and followed up with a survey to determine the most common barriers that can undermine female professionals and reinforce the glass ceiling. This extensive research created the foundation for the survey.

The survey examines three types of barriers: individual, organization, and transitional barriers. Each of these barriers captures a grouping of sub-barriers stopping women from moving into leadership roles.

Individual Barriers

- *Personal Life:* assesses if women think it is difficult to combine a more senior role with their personal commitments.
- *Self-Promotion:* assesses women's propensity to create their own barriers in their professional lives.

- *Societal Expectations:* assesses how social and cultural norms affect women's decision-making.
- *Awareness:* assesses the level of women's recognition of the benefits and rewards that can come from taking the next career step.

Organizational Barriers

- *Performance Evaluation:* assesses women's perception of how their performance is valued and how their capabilities are rated in the organization.
- *Management Attitude:* assesses what the perceived attitude of management is toward women aspiring to actively move ahead in the organization.
- *Organizational Support:* assesses how the organization backs women to move up.

Transitional Barriers

- *Support Network:* assesses the strength of supportive relationships in the women's professional life.
- *Manage Issues:* assesses women's ability to make decisions in unclear circumstances, their ability to rapid prototype to arrive at solutions, and their ability to manage conflict in order to resolve issues.
- *Resilience:* assesses women's ability to stay calm under pressure and to manage stress effectively.
- *Manage Yourself:* assesses women's level of individual awareness and their ability to quell negative thoughts and replace them with positive thinking and action.

The stronger the barriers are, the greater the risk index score. The risk index score measures the risk of organizations losing female talent from the leadership pipeline, either because they give up or because they leave the organization to find better opportunities elsewhere. Each barrier has an equal share in the overall risk index.

Participant Profile

A total of 1,075 women participated in this survey. The results were based on their answers. Below are the highlights of the participant profile.

Industry Sectors

Participants represented 24 different industry sectors.

- 9% finance/insurance
- 9% public administration
- 8% manufacturing
- 8% professional services

Job Areas

Participants represented 19 different job areas.

- 13% HR
- 11% General management
- 12% Consultant

Size of the Organization

- 63% large
- 12% medium
- 25% small

Country of Residence

- 74% European Union (mainly France and Belgium)
- 3% USA
- 23% rest of the world

Are You Member of a Women's/Diversity Network in Your Organization?

- 36% yes
- 64% no

Age

- 19% were between ages of 18–35
- 32% were between ages of 36–45
- 47% were between ages of 46–65
- 2% were 65 and over

Family Situation—Children

- 33% No
- 10% Yes, infants (0–three years)
- 37% Yes, school ages (four–18 years)
- 25% Yes, older than 18 years

Childcare Responsibility

- 39% complete
- 14% partial
- 2% weekend only
- 45% no children at home

Family Responsibility Shared with Partner

- 43% we share equally
- 40% we share, but I do more than partner
- 10% we share, but partner does more than I do 6 percent we do not share, I do most
- 1% we do not share, my partner does most of it

Expatriate (WiSER) Research Details

Research Details

Research Hypotheses

We started our research with two hypotheses:

(a) There are shared global leader competencies among WiSER.
   As we began our research, we measured and coded for six competencies which we thought would be prevalent among WiSER based on initial interviews. Those competencies were:
   - operating outside your comfort zone,
   - active career management,
   - conscious imbalance,
   - energy management,
   - self-awareness,
   - creativity.
(b) An international assignment will enhance your professional career.

Research Method

We interviewed 62 women who all held a C-level, executive, or emerging executive role. The WiSER lived and worked abroad for at least one year. Interviews were conducted during the period February 2011–February 2012, either over the phone or in person and lasted approximately between 60 and 90 minutes. All interviews were audio-recorded and transcribed by a third party. The WiSER also completed an online survey to capture demographic data relating to personal and professional life and specific to their expatriate assignment(s).

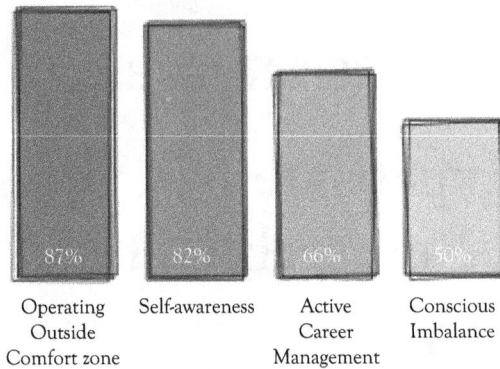

87%	82%	66%	50%
Operating	Self-awareness	Active	Conscious
Outside		Career	Imbalance
Comfort zone		Management	

Figure B.1 WiSER competencies

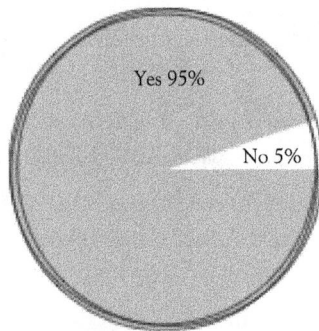

Yes 95%

No 5%

Figure B.2 Was career enhanced by international assignment?

Research Results

The qualitative analysis of the data revealed that four competencies were observable at a greater and significant percentage (Figure B.1). Those are the WiSER competencies explored in the book.

When asked, 95 percent of WiSER answered that an international assignment enhanced their career (Figure B.2).

WiSER Profile

Life-related Demographics

The WiSER were single, married, or divorced; with and without children; aged between 25 and 60; representing six of the seven continents, with only Antarctica not represented.

Countries of Origin

- Australia (1), Belgium (2), Brazil (2), Canada (3), Denmark (1), Egypt (1), Finland (1), Germany (5), Holland (5), India (3), Ireland (1), Israel (1), Italy (1), Jamaica (1), Macedonia (1), Northern Ireland (1), South Africa (1), Sweden (1), Turkey (1), UK (5), USA (17), not reported (7)

Nationalities

- Australia (1), Belgium (2), Brazil (2), Canada (1), Denmark (1), Finland (1), Germany (4), Holland (5), India (1), Ireland (1), Israel (1), Italy (1), Singapore (1), South Africa (1), Sweden (2), Turkey (1), UK (3), USA (19), dual citizenship (7), not reported (7)

Age at Time of Interview

- WiSER's age ranged from 25 to 60
- 13% were between ages of 30–39
- 42% were between ages of 40–49
- 24% were between ages of 50–59
- 3% were 60 and over
- 18% did not report their age

Civil Status

Marital status at time of interview

- 81% were either married or in a serious relationship
- 5% were single, never married
- 11% were either divorced or widowed
- 3% not evident

Family Status at Time of Expatriate Assignment

- 63% had children while on international assignment
- 34% did not have children either before or during their international assignment(s)

- 3% did not report
- Twice as many women had children while on international assignment than those who did not have children
- 56% were married/in a serious relationship and had children while on an international assignment

Partner Information at Time of International Assignment (Based on 50 WiSER Who Had a Partner at the Time of their Assignment)

- 58% of partners worked in the host country
- 18% of partners did not work in host country
- 10% of partners did not relocate to host country
- 14% not evident

Miscellaneous

- 45% had first international experience as child or teenager
- 77% expressed desire to live abroad before their first international assignment
- 34% of all WiSER (regardless of SIE or OIE) had one or both parents who were immigrants

Work-Related Demographics

The WiSER have a wealth of experience but also a variety of experience in multiple organizations. We validated their seniority based on various criteria, including but not limited to title, span of control (number of staff and geographical responsibility), salary, and budget managed. The level of expertise in this sample was high and reputable.

Expat Experience

Expat Locations

- A total of 150 international assignments spread among the 62 WiSER

- Countries of expat locations: Australia (3) , Austria (1), Bangladesh (1), Belgium (3), Burundi (1), Cambodia (1), Cameroon (1), Canada (3), China (4), Czech Republic (4), Ecuador (1), Egypt (1), El Salvador (1), Finland (3), France (3), Germany (16), Hong Kong (4) UK (14), Hungary (1), India (3), Indonesia (2), Iraq (1), Italy (3), Japan (2), Kenya (4), Liberia (1), Malaysia (2), Mali (1), Mexico (3), Monaco (1), Mongolia (3), Mozambique (1), Nepal (1), Netherlands (3), Nicaragua (1), Panama (2), Papua New Guinea (1), Paraguay (1), Peru (1), Poland (2), Romania (1), Russia (2), Singapore (6), Slovakia (1), Somalia (1), South Africa (2), South Korea (2), Spain (3), Sudan (1), Switzerland (6), Taiwan (1), Thailand (1), UAE (2), USA (14), Venezuela (1), Yemen (1)

Expatriate Experience

- 21% had five or more international assignments
- 29% had three–four international assignments
- 50% had one–two international assignments
- 60% had first international assignment when junior professional
- 27% had first international assignment as senior professional
- 11% got first international assignment as intern
- 2% not evident
- 71% were expatriated through organization (OIE)
- 26% self-initiated their expatriation (SIE)
- 3% had both experiences

Selection for First Expatriate Assignment (Based on 56 Responses; Multiple Answers Were Possible)

- 23% actively selected to work for a global employer in the hope of an international opportunity
- 11% only applied for international opportunities
- 34% actively informed my employer of my interest in international opportunities

- 36% were presented with an international opportunity by employer
- 23% were recruited for an international opportunity

Length of Expatriate Experience

- 45% 1–3 years
- 29% 4–6 years
- 21% 7–12 years
- 5% 13+ years

Length of Time in Organization Prior to Obtaining Most Recent Expatriate Assignment (Based on 30 Responses)

- 33% worked in organization 1–3 years
- 30% worked in organization 4–6 years
- 17% worked in organization 7–9 years
- 20% worked in organization 10+ years

General Experience

General Work Experience at Time of Interview

- 9% had less than 12 years of experience
- 16% had 13–16 years of experience
- 16% had 17–19 years of experience
- 59% had 20+ years of experience

Function at Time of Most Recent International Assignment

- 19% had a cross-functional position
- 24% worked in the area of human resources
- WiSER represented 11 different functional areas. In addition to HR, the following functional areas were represented: business development, communications, finance, information technology, insurance, legal, manufacturing, marketing, operations, and research.

Mentors/Sponsors at Time of Interview

- 85% had one or more mentors/sponsors in their career
- 40% of mentors/sponsors were male
- 14% had female mentors/sponsors
- 23% had both male and female mentors/sponsors
- 23% not evident if WiSER had only male, only female, or both male and female mentors/sponsors

Seniority

Salary in USD

Only includes base pay and bonus. Health benefits, stock options, housing allowance, COLA, school tuitions, and other fringe benefits are not included.

- 18% earned $75,000–$125,000
- 41% earned $125,000–$225,000
- 26% earned $225,000–$300,000
- 15% earned > $300,000

Job level *(based on 49 answers to the question, how many levels down was the job from a chief level position?)*

- 20% were C-level (0 levels down)
- 51% were Executive (1–3 levels down)
- 29% were emerging executive (4–6 levels down)

Budget Responsibility (Based on 34 answers)

- 53% = <$ 15M
- 6% = $15.1M–$100M
- 15% = $101M–$500M
- 18% = $501M–$1B
- 9% = >$1.1B

Organization Profile

Sector at Time of Interview

- 69% worked for a for-profit organization
- 15% worked for a non-profit organization
- 13% worked for a governmental organization
- 3% were self-employed

Industry at Time of Most Recent International Assignment

WiSER worked in 19 different industries (Figure B.3)

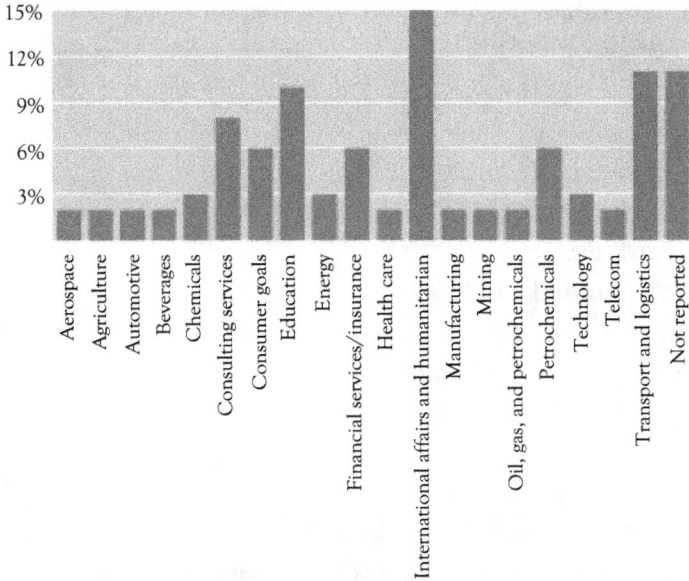

Figure B.3 Industry at time of most recent international assignment

Organizations

Table B.1 Sample set of world class organizations WiSER are (or were) employed with

Adecco	Have Faith In Your Brand
Added Value	ING
Arthur Anderson	Johnson & Johnson
Association for the Advancement of	The ISTAR Group
International Education (AAIE)	Kuehne+Nagel
Astra Zeneca	LEGO
Baxter	Lloyds of London
Bayer	Medtronic
Brio International	Mylanda
CGIAR	NASA
Child Fund International	Open Society Foundations
Coca Cola	Orrekel English
Deloitte & Touche	Pfizer
Deutsche Telekom	Procter & Gamble
Deutsche Post-DHL	Randstad
Dow Chemical	Rio Tinto
Dow Corning	Russell Reynolds
Dow Jones	Samsung
Eli Lilly	Shell
Fairtrade International	Siemens
General Electric	Sommer Consulting
General Motors	United Nations

Bibliography

Achor, S. 2018. "Do Women's Networking Events Move the Needle on Equality?" *Harvard Business Review*, February 13. https://hbr.org/2018/02/do-womens-networking-events-move-the-needle-on-equality (accessed May 21, 2018).

American Management Association. 2008. "Expatriate Assignments are on the Rise." http://amanet.org/training/articles/expatriate-assignments-are-on-the-rise.aspx (accessed November 25, 2012).

Anderson, S., and J. Cavanaugh. 2000. "Top 200: The Rise of Corporate Global Power." *Institute for Policy Studies*. http://ips-dc.org/reports/top_200_the_rise_of_corporate_global_power (accessed October 31, 2012).

Andors, A. 2010. "Happy Returns: The Success of Repatriating Expatriate Employees Requires Forethought and Effective Management." *SHRM* 55, no. 3, pp. 3–10. http://shrm.org/Publications/hrmagazine/EditorialContent/2010/0310/Pages/0310agenda_relocation.aspx (accessed November 21, 2012).

Audia, P. 2009. "A New B-school Specialty: Self-Awareness." *Forbes.com*, http://forbes.com/2009/12/04/tuck-self-awareness-leadership-careers-education.html (accessed November 21, 2012).

Berard, J. 2012. "Power of Self-Awareness." *Global Knowledge*. http://blog.globalknowledge.co.uk/2012/08/24/the-power-of-self-awareness (accessed November 21, 2012).

BGRS. 2016. "2016 Global Mobility Trends Survey-Breakthrough to the Future of Global Talent Mobility." http://globalmobilitytrends.bgrs.com/assets2016/downloads/Full-Report-BGRS-2016-Global-Mobility-Trends-Survey.pdf (accessed June 23, 2018).

Bhargava, R. 2012. *Likeonomics: The Unexpected Truth Behind Earning Trust, Influencing Behavior, and Inspiring Action*. Hoboken, New Jersey: John Wiley & Sons.

Blumberg, Y. 2018. "Companies with More Female Executives Make More Money—Here's Why/By Yoni Blumberg." *CNBC.com*, March 2. https://cnbc.com/2018/03/02/why-companies-with-female-managers-make-more-money.html (accessed August 15, 2018).

Boatman, J., and R.S. Wellins. 2011. "Global Leadership Forecast 2011." *DDI World*. http://ddiworld.com/glf (accessed November 21, 2012).

Bradberry, T., and J. Greaves. 2005. *The Emotional Intelligence Quickbook: Everything You Need to Know to Put Your EQ to Work*. New York, NY: Simon & Schuster.

Brookfield Global Relocation Services. 2012. "The 2012 Global Relocation Trends Survey Report Highlights." http://knowledge.brookfieldgrs.com/content/insights_ideas-2012_GRTS (accessed November 21, 2012).

Buckingham, M. 2009. *Find Your Strongest Life: What the Happiest and Most Successful Women do Differently*. Nashville, TN: Thomas Nelson.

Carter, N.M., and C. Silva. 2011. "The Myth of the Ideal Worker: Does Doing All the Right Things Really Get Women Ahead?" *Catalyst*, http://catalyst.org/knowledge/myth-ideal-worker-does-doing-all-right-things-really-get-women-ahead (accessed November 19, 2012).

Catalyst. 2000. "Passport to Opportunity: U.S. Women in Global Business." http://catalyst.org/publication/78/passport-to-opportunity-us-women-in-global-business (accessed November 21, 2012).

Catalyst. 2009. "Men's Support Crucial to Creating Gender Diversity in the Workplace." *Catalyst.org*, May 13. https://catalyst.org/system/files/Engaging_Men_In_Gender_Initiatives_What_Change_Agents_Need_To_Know.pdf (accessed May 15, 2018).

Center for Women and Business at Bentley University. 2017. *Men as Allies. Engaging Men to Advance Women in the Workplace*, https://bentley.edu/files/2017/05/02/CWB%20Men%20as%20Allies%20Research%20Report%20Spring%202017.pdf (accessed September 17, 2018).

Cohen, P. 2017. "Why Women Quit Working: It's Not for the Reasons Men Do." *NYTimes.com*, January 14. https://nytimes.com/2017/01/24/business/economy/women-labor-force.html (accessed May 14, 2018).

Collins, J. 2001. *Good to Great*. New York, NY: HarperCollins Publishers.

Conference Board. 2018. "CEO Challenge Study 2018." *25 Research Insights to Fuel Your People Strategy. Ey.com*, https://ey.com/Publication/vwLUAssets/ey-the-global-leadership-forecast/$FILE/ey-the-global-leadership-forecast.pdf (accessed August 21, 2018).

Correll, S., and C. Simard. 2016. "Research: Vague Feedback is Holding Women Back." *HBR.com*, April 29. https://hbr.org/2016/04/research-vague-feedback-is-holding-women-back (accessed June 16, 2018).

Covey, S. "How the Best Leaders Build Trust." *Leadershipnow.com* https://leadershipnow.com/CoveyOnTrust.html (accessed September 17, 2018).

Credit Suisse. 2012. "Gender Diversity and Corporate Performance." https://infocus.credit-suisse.com/data/_product_documents/_shop/360145/csri_gender_diversity_and_corporate_performance.pdf (accessed January 22, 2013).

Cross, R., A. Cowen, L. Vertucci, and R.J. Thomas. 2009. "Leading in a Connected World: How Effective Leaders Drive Results Through Networks." University of Virginia. http://robcross.org/pdf/research/leading_in_connected_world.pdf (accessed December 10, 2012).

Curtin, M. 2017. "Science: Companies With Women in Top Management Are Much More Profitable." *Inc.com*, May 31. https://inc.com/melanie-curtin/science-companies-with-women-in-top-management-are-significantly-more-profitable.html (accessed June 16, 2018).

De Paula, L., and S. Ondraschek-Norris. 2016. *JUMP.eu.com*, September 20. http://jump.eu.com/men-still-holding-back-championing-gender-equality/ (accessed August 29, 2018).

Dewar J. 2018. "Where Unconscious Bias Creeps into the Recruitment Process." *Recruiting Brief,* July 26. https://bit.ly/2sakHOb (accessed August 5, 2018).

Dishman, L. 2018. "What is the Glass Cliff, and Why do So Many Female CEOs Fall Off It?" *Fastcompany.com*, July 21. https://fastcompany.com/90206067/what-is-the-glass-cliff-and-why-do-so-many-female-ceos-fall-off-it (accessed August 7, 2018).

Dizik, A. 2016. "Where are All the Expat Women?" *BBC.com*, September 30. http://bbc.com/capital/story/20160929-where-are-all-the-expat-women (accessed August 19, 2018).

DOL (Department of Labor). 2011. "Women's Employment During the Recovery." http://dol.gov/_sec/media/reports/FemaleLaborForce/Female LaborForce.pdf (accessed March 17, 2010).

Donaldson, C. 2017. "Leveraging Diversity to Improve the Customer Experience." *Inc.com*, February 20. https://insidehr.com.au/use-diversity-improve-innovation-customer-experience/ (accessed June 5, 2018).

Dulworth, M. 2008. *The Connect Effect*. San Francisco, California: Berett-Koehler Publishers, Inc.

Economist Intelligence Unit Ltd. 2010. "Up or Out. Next Moves for the Modern Expatriate." *The Economist*, http://graphics.eiu.com/upload/eb/LON_PL_Regus_WEB2.pdf (accessed July 2, 2018).

Economy, Peter. 2014. "The 9 Traits That Define Great Leadership." *Inc.com*, January 24. https://inc.com/peter-economy/the-9-traits-that-define-great-leadership.html (accessed June 7, 2018).

Edmonson, A. 2014. "Building a Psychologically Safe Workplace." *Youtube.com*, May 4. https://youtube.com/watch?v=LhoLuui9gX8 (accessed May 7, 2018).

Europa. 2011. "EU Justice Commissioner Viviane Reding Meeting European Business Leaders to Push for More Women in Boardrooms." *Press Release*, January 3. http://europa.eu/rapid/press-release_IP-11-242_en.htm (accessed November 21, 2012).

Expat Explorer. 2012. "What is Culture Shock?" April 24. http://expatexplorer.blogspot.co.uk/2012/04/what-is-culture-shock.html (accessed November 21, 2012).

Expatica. 2008. "Women on Assignment: An Evolutionary Perspective." http://expatica.com/pt/employment/employment_information/Women-assignment_-An-evolutionary-perspective_11545.html (accessed November 21, 2012).

Federal Glass Ceiling Commission. 1995. "A Solid Investment: Making Full use of the Nation's Human Capital." http://dol.gov/oasam/programs/history/reich/reports/ceiling2.pdf (accessed January 8, 2013).

Foust-Cummings, H., S. Dinolfo, and J. Kohler. 2011. "Sponsoring Women to Success." *Catalyst*, http://catalyst.org/file/497/sponsoring_women_to_success.pdf (accessed November 19, 2012).

George, B. 2011. "Leadership Skills Start with Self-Awareness." *Star Tribune*, February 26. http://startribune.com/business/116923928.html?refer=y (accessed November 21, 2012).

Giles, S. 2016. "The Most Important Leadership Competencies, According to Leaders Around the World." *HBR.org*, March 15. https://hbr.org/2016/03/the-most-important-leadership-competencies-according-to-leaders-around-the-world (accessed July 10, 2018).

Goldin, C., and C. Rouse. 1997. "Orchestrating Impartiality: The Impact of "Blind" Auditions on Female Musicians." *National Bureau of Economic Research*, http://nber.org/papers/w5903 (accessed January 13, 2013).

Goleman, D. October 4, 2015. http://danielgoleman.info/daniel-goleman-how-self-awareness-impacts-your-work/ (accessed August 18, 2018).

Hallowell, W., and C. Grove. 1997. "Female Assignees: Lessons Learned." *Runzheimer International*, http://grovewell.com/pub-expat-females.html (accessed November 20, 2012).

Hallowell, W., and C. Grove. 1997. "Guidelines for Women Expatriates." *InterMedia Solutions*, Inc. http://grovewell.com/pub-expat-women.html (accessed November 20, 2012).

Haslberger, A. August 6-8, 2007. "Gender Differences in Expatriate Adjustment." Paper, presented at the 67th Annual Meeting of the Academy of Management, Philadelphia.

Herway, J. 2017. "How to Create a Culture of Psychological Safety." *Gallup.com*, December 7. https://gallup.com/workplace/236198/create-culture-psychological-safety.aspx (accessed June 19, 2018).

Hogan, T. 2009. "Global Talent Management and Global Mobility." *Mobility*. http://worldwideerc.org/Resources/MOBILITYarticles/Pages/0209hogan.aspx (accessed November 20, 2012).

Hoogendoorn, S., H. Oosterbeek, and M. Praag van. 2013. "The Impact of Gender Diversity on the Performance of Business Teams: Evidence from a Field Experiment." *Management Science* 59, no. 7, pp. 1514–28.

Huston, T. 2016. "We are Way Harder on Female Leaders Who Make Bad Calls." *HBR.org*, 21 April. https://hbr.org/2016/04/research-we-are-way-harder-on-female-leaders-who-make-bad-calls (accessed August 9, 2018).

Ibarra, H., N.M. Carter, and C. Silva. 2010. "Why Men Still Get More Promotions than Women." *Harvard Business Review*. http://hbr.org/2010/09/why-men-still-get-more-promotions-than-women/ar/1 (accessed November 19, 2012).

Independent. 2017. "Women do More Household Chores than Men, Study Finds." *Independent.co.uk*, 27 September. https://www.independent.co.uk/life-style/women-household-chores-men-do-more-gender-inequality-home-study-a7969306.html (accessed November 26, 2018).

Iowa State University. 2012. "Self-Awareness: The Essence of Effective Leadership." http://blogs.extension.iastate.edu/hr/2012/04/16/self-awareness-the-essence-of-effective-leadership/ (accessed November 21, 2012).

Javidan, M., M. Teagarden, F. Babrinde, K. Walch, N. Lynton, C. Pearson, D. Bowen, and A. Cabrera. 2007. "Global Mindset Defined: Expat Success Strategy." *Mobility*, http://worldwideerc.org/Foundation/Documents/global_mindset.pdf (accessed November 19, 2012).

Javidan, M., M. Teagarden, and D. Bowen. 2010. "Making it Overseas." *Harvard Business Review*, http://asaecenter.org/files/FileDownloads/HandOuts/2011 International/Making%20it%20Overseas%20-%20HBR%20 -%20Thunderbird%20University%20-%20provided%20by%20 StrategicStraits%20Inc..pdf (accessed November 19, 2012).

Javidan, M. 2010. "Bringing the Global Mindset to Leadership." *HBR Blog Network*. http://blogs.hbr.org/imagining-the-future-of-leadership/2010/05/bringing-the-global-mindset-to.html (accessed November 21, 2012).

Javidan, M. 2010. "The Skills You Need to Lead Overseas." *Interview. HBR IdeaCast*, March 25. http://blogs.hbr.org/ideacast/2010/03/the-skills-you-need-to-lead-ov.html (accessed November 21, 2012).

Jobvite. 2011. "Jobvite Survey." *Social Job Seeker Survey* 2011. http://recruiting.jobvite.com/resources/social-recruiting-reports-and-trends/ (accessed November 21, 2012).

Jordan, J., and S. Cartwright. 1998. "Selecting Expatriate Managers: Key Traits and Competencies." *Leadership & Organization Development Journal* 19, no. 2, pp. 89–96.

Kelly, M. 2011. *Off Balance: Getting Beyond the Work-Life Balance Myth to Personal and Professional Satisfaction*. New York, NY: Hudson Street Press.

Keys, D. T., and R.S. Wellins. 2008. "DNA of a Global Leader: There is a Certain Strategy that Needs to be Addressed to Create Global Leaders." *T + D*. http://66.179.232.89/pdf/T+Dreprint_March08.pdf (accessed November 21, 2012).

Kohls, L.R. 2001. *Survival Kit for Overseas Living: For Americans Planning to Work and Live Abroad*. Boston/ London: Nicholas Brealey Publishing.

Langley, S. 2012. "The Neuroscience of Change: Why it's Difficult and What Makes it Easier By Sue Langley." *Langleygroup.com*, May 23. http://blog. langleygroup.com.au/neuroscience-of-change-what-makes-change-easier/ (accessed June 27, 2018).

Lebowitz, S. 2015. "Google Considers This to Be the Most Critical Trait of Successful Teams." *Businessinsider.com*, November 20. https://businessinsider. com/amy-edmondson-on-psychological-safety-2015-11 (accessed June 24, 2018).

Levensaler, L. 2016. "How Tomorrow's Leaders Will Survive The Storm." July 14. https://forbes.com/sites/workday/2016/07/14/how-tomorrows-leaders-will-survive-the-storm/#4e3e43f52c53 (accessed July 5, 2018).

Linehan, M., and H. Scullion. 2001. "European Female Expatriate Careers: Critical Success Factors." *Journal of European Industrial Training* 25, no. 8, pp. 392–418.

Linehan, M., and H. Scullion. 2008. "The Development of Female Global Managers: The Role of Mentoring and Networking." *Journal of Business Ethics* 83, no. 1, pp. 29–40.

Loehr, J., and T. Schwartz. 2003. *The Power of Full Engagement*. New York, NY: The Free Press.

Lorenzo, R., N. Voigt, K. Schetelig, A. Zawadzki, I. Welpe, and P. Brosi. 2017. "The Mix that Matters-Innovation Through Diversity." April 26. https://bcg. com/publications/2017/people-organization-leadership-talent-innovation-through-diversity-mix-that-matters.aspx (accessed July 17, 2018).

Lui, R. March 6, 2014. "The Crucial Role of Men in Gender Equality." *MSNBC*. NBC Universal News Group.

Luxton, E. 2016. "Why Managers Give Women Less Feedback." *Weforum.org*, October 20. https://weforum.org/agenda/2016/10/managers-give-women-less-feedback/ (accessed September 3, 2018).

Maertz, C.P., A. Hassan, and P. Magnusson. 2009. "When Learning is Not Enough: A Process Model of Expatriate Adjustment as Cultural Cognitive Dissonance Reduction." *Organizational Behaviors and Human Decision Processes* 108, no. 1, pp. 66–78.

McKinsey & Company. 2007. "Women Matter: Gender Diversity, A Corporate Performance Driver." http://mckinsey.de/downloads/publikation/women_matter/Women_Matter_1_brochure.pdf (accessed November 21, 2012).

McKinsey & Company. 2010. "Women at the Top of Corporations: Making it Happen." http://mckinsey.com/features/women_matter (accessed November 21, 2012).

McKinsey & Company. 2012. "The World at Work: Jobs, Pay and Skills for 3.5 Billion People." http://mckinsey.com/insights/mgi/research/labor_markets/the_world_at_work (accessed November 21, 2012).

McKinsey & Company. 2016. "Women Matter 2016. Reinventing the Workplace to Unlock the Potential of Gender Diversity." https://mck.co/2CQ9ys5 (accessed February 2, 2018).

McLaren, S. 2018. "These Industries Will Face the Biggest Talent Shortages by 2030." *Linkedin.com*, July 24, 2018. https://business.linkedin.com/talent-solutions/blog/trends-and-research/2018/industries-biggest-talent-shortages-2030 (accessed August 12, 2018).

Mercer. 2018. "Alternative International Assignments Survey." *Mercer.com*, https://imercer.com/ecommerce/products/Alternative-International-Assignments-Survey (accessed September 14, 2018).

Mo, H., and J.M. Xia. 2010. "A Preliminary Research on Self-Initiated Expatriation as Compared to Assigned Expatriation." *Canadian Social Science* 6, no. 5, pp. 169–77.

Musselwhite, C. 2007. "Self-awareness and the Effective Leader." *Inc.com*, http://inc.com/resources/leadership/articles/20071001/musselwhite.html (accessed November 21, 2012).

Noland Y., T. Moran, and B. Kotschwar. 2016. "Is Gender Diversity Profitable? Evidence from a Global Survey." *Piie.com*, https://piie.com/system/files/documents/wp16-3.pdf (accessed October 13, 2018).

NWLink. 2012. "70-20-10: Is it a Viable Learning Model?" http://nwlink.com/~donclark/hrd/media/70-20-10.html (accessed January 23, 2013).

Oberg, L. 2012. "Culture Shock and the Problem of Adjustment to New Cultural Environments." *Worldwide Classroom*, http://worldwide.edu/travel_planner/culture_shock.html (accessed November 19, 2012).

Peters, H., and R. Kabacoff. 1998/2010. "A New Look at the Glass Ceiling: The Perspective from the Top." *Workinfo.com*, http://workinfo.com/free/downloads/136.htm (accessed October 31, 2012).

Petriglieri, G. 2014. "There Is No Shortage of Leaders." *HBR.com*, December 15. https://hbr.org/2014/12/there-is-no-shortage-of-leaders (accessed August 17, 2018).

PEW Social Trends. 2015. "Public Says Women are Equally Qualified, But Barriers Persist." *Pewsocialtrends.org*, January 15. http://pewsocialtrends.org/2015/01/14/women-and-leadership/ (accessed July 2, 2018).

Phillips, K., R. Lount, O. Sheldon, and F. Rink. "The Biases That Punish Racially Diverse Teams." *HBR.com*, February 22. https://hbr.org/2016/02/the-biases-that-punish-racially-diverse-teams (accessed August 9, 2018).

PriceWaterhouseCoopers. 2007. "Women's Economic Participation: Enablers, Barriers, Responses." http://pwc.com/en_GX/gx/women-at-pwc/assets/pwc_genesis_park_report.pdf (accessed November 21, 2012).

PriceWaterhouseCoopers. 2016. "Moving Women with Purpose." *Creating Gender Inclusive Global Mobility*. https://pwc.com/gx/en/diversity-inclusion/

assets/moving-women-with-purpose-executive-summary.pdf (accessed September 18, 2018).

Pucik V., and T. Saba. 1998. "Selecting and Developing the Global Versus the Expatriate Manager: A Review of the State of the Art." *Human Resource Planning* 21, no. 4, p. 40.

Reed, J., and R. Cook. 2012. "Women in the Global Business World: Identifying the Myths." *Global Excellence*, http://global-excellence.com/women-expatriates.php (accessed November 21, 2012).

Reed J., and R. Cook. 2012. "Women and Safety in a Global Business World: Deconstructing Myth 2." *Global Excellence*, http://global-excellence.com/women-expatriates.php (accessed November 21, 2012).

Reed J., and R. Cook. 2012. "Can women Expatriates Handle Work and Family Abroad? Deconstructing Myth 3." *Global Excellence*, http://global-excellence.com/women-expatriates.php (accessed November 21, 2012).

Reiche, S. 2011. "Do International Assignments Add Walue to Your Career?" *IESE*, http://blog.iese.edu/expatriatus/2011/08/23/do-international-assignments-add-value-to-your-career/ (accessed November 21, 2012).

Roberts, E. 2016. "More Women Using Expat Postings to Fast-Track their Careers." https://telegraph.co.uk/expat/expatlife/12115571/More-women-using-expat-postings-to-fast-track-their-careers.html (accessed August 2, 2018).

Rock, D. 2009. "Managing with the Brain in Mind." *Strategy + Business*, http://davidrock.net/files/ManagingWBrainInMind.pdf (accessed November 20, 2012).

Schachter, H. 2011. "Why Mindset can Trump Skill Set." *Globe and Mail*, July 4. http://theglobeandmail.com/report-on-business/careers/management/why-mindset-can-trump-skill-set/article615652/ (accessed November 21, 2012).

Schoemaker, P.J.H. 2011. *Brilliant Mistakes: Finding Success in the Far Side of Failure*. Philadelphia: Wharton Digital Press.

Scivicque, C. "Career Management: Defining the Process and Purpose." *Careerealism*, http://careerealism.com/career-management-defining-process-purpose/ (accessed November 13, 2012).

Selmer, J., and J. Lauring. 2015. "Host Country Language Ability and Expatriate Adjustment: The Moderating Effect of Language Difficulty." *International Journal of Human Resource Management* 26, no. 3, pp. 401–20.

Shaffer, M.A., D.A. Harrison, H. Gregersen, J.S. Black, and L.A. Ferzandi. 2006. "You Can Take It with You: Individual Differences and Expatriate Effectiveness." *Journal of Applied Psychology* 91, no. 1, pp. 109–25.

Shen, L. 2018. "What's Stopping Female Jobseekers From Landing Interviews? Their 'A' Grades, Says Study." May 3. https://bit.ly/2F6ZXi8 (accessed June 25, 2018).

Shortland, S., and Y. Altman. 2007. "Expats Average 13.4 More Work Hours Per Week Over Home Location." *SHRM*, http://shrm.org/hrdisciplines/global/Articles/Pages/CMS_023198.aspx (accessed February 22, 2012).

Shortland, S., and Y. Altman. 2011. "What do We Really Know About Corporate Career Women Expatriates?" *European International Management* 5, no. 3, pp. 209–34. http://shrm.org/hrdisciplines/global/Articles/Pages/CMS_018746.aspx (accessed November 21, 2012).

SHRM (Society for Human Resource Management). 2004. "Emerging Trends in Global Mobility: The Assignee Perspective." *2004 Worldwide Benchmark Study*, http://shrm.org/Research/SurveyFindings/Documents/Emerging%20Trends%20in%20Global%20Mobility%20-%20A%20Study%20by%20SHRM%20and%20Willamette%20University.pdf (accessed November 21, 2012).

SHRM (Society for Human Resource Management). 2008. "Selected Cross-cultural Factors in Human Resource Management." *SHRM Research Quarterly. Third Quarter*, http://shrm.org/Research/Articles/Documents/September%202008%20Research%20Quarterly%20-%20Selected%20Cross-Cultural%20Factors%20in%20Human%20Resource%20Management.pdf (accessed November 21, 2012).

SHRM (Society for Human Resource Management). 2008. "Leadership Competencies." http://shrm.org/Research/Articles/Articles/PagesLeadership Competencies.aspx (accessed January 9, 2013).

Spencer, S.T. 2007. *The Art of Crossing Cultures*, 2nd ed. Boston/London: Nicholas Brealey Publishing.

Spencer, S.T. 2011. "Briefcase Essentials for Women in Business." *Knowledge@Wharton*, May 19. http://knowledge.wharton.upenn.edu/article.cfm?article id=2782 (accessed November 21, 2012).

Tessman, D., and R. Wellins. 2008. "DNA of a Global Leader." *ASTD*, http://astd.org/Publications/Magazines/TD/TD-Archive/2008/03/DNA-of-a-Global-Leader. (accessed January 22, 2013).

Thunderbird School of Global Management. 2012. "GMI for Executives and Corporation." http://globalmindset.thunderbird.edu/home/global-mindset-inventory/assessment-executives-corporations (accessed November 21, 2012).

Thurmon, D. 2010. *Off Balance on Purpose*. Austin, TX: Greenleaf Book Group Press.

Trompenaars, F., and C. Hampden-Turner. 2006. *Riding the Waves of Culture: Understanding Cultural Diversity in Business*. London: Nicholas Brealey Publishing.

Tull, M. 2009. "Risk-Taking." *About.com*, http://ptsd.about.com/od/glossary/g/risktaking.htm (accessed November 21, 2012).

Tung, R.L. 2005. "Can Women Succeed as Global Managers?" *Executive Education*. China Europe International Business School E-Newsletter iDEA. http://ceibs.edu/pdf/execed/e.inspire1.womensc.pdf (accessed October 31, 2012).

Tungli, Z., and M. Peiperl. 2008. "Expatriate Practices in German, Japanese, UK and US Multinational Companies: A Comparative Survey of Changes." *Human Resource Management* 48, no. 1, pp. 153–71.

Tyler, K. 2001. "Don't Fence her in: Outdated Assumptions About Spouses, Safety and Culture may Prompt Managers to Pass Over Women for International Jobs." *HR Magazine*, http://shrm.org/Publications/hrmagazine/EditorialContent/0301/Pages/0301tyler.aspx (accessed October 31, 2012).

Tyler, K. 2006. "Retraining Repatriates." *HR Magazine*, http://shrm.org/publications/hrmagazine/editorialcontent/pages/0306agenda_global.aspx (accessed October 31, 2012).

Vance C., Y. McNulty, and F. Chauderlot. 2011. "Unpublished Manuscript." *A Comparison of Female and Male Strategies for Securing and Enduring Expatriate Career Development Experiences*.

Wanberg, C.R., J. Zhu, D.A. Harrison, and E.W. Diehn. 2011. "Crossing Cultures: Unpacking the Expatriate Learning and Adjustment Process." *SHRM Foundation*, http://shrm.org/about/foundation/research/Documents/Wanberg%20Exec%20Summary%206-11.pdf (accessed November 21, 2012).

White, A.K. 2009. *From Comfort Zone to Performance Management*. La Houlette, Belgium.

Williams, J., R. Dempsey, and A. Slaughter. 2014. *What Works for Women at Work: Four Patterns Working Women Need to Know*. New York, NY: New York University Press.

Zarya, V. 2018. "The Share of Female CEOs in the Fortune 500 Dropped by 25% in 2018." *Fortune.com*, http://fortune.com/2018/05/21/women-fortune-500-2018/ (accessed September 15, 2018).

Zenger, J., and J. Folkman. 2012. "Are Women Better Leaders than Men?" *HBR. org*, March 15. https://hbr.org/2012/03/a-study-in-leadership-women-do (accessed September 9, 2018).

About the Authors

Sapna Welsh and Caroline Kersten are founding partners of Leverage HR where they transition diverse talent to the top. Their team of leadership coaches and facilitators support diversity and inclusion efforts across the US and Europe through leadership coaching, facilitation, consulting, and workshops. They have trained and coached high potential talent with some of the most notable Fortune 500, Fortune 1000 organizations, and NGOs. Whether you are seeking to manage your career, find new sources of energy and focus, or want to improve performance and impact, Leverage HR focuses on inspiring their clients to leverage their talents to maximize their personal leadership and achieve their goals.

Sapna Welsh holds a master's degree in human resources from The Ohio State University, and a BBA in international business from The George Washington University. She is a licensed HR professional, a registered corporate coach, and certified in various psychometric tools.

Caroline Kersten holds a master's degrees in European studies and Dutch law from the University of Amsterdam, and an LLM in European law from the College of Europe Bruges. She has lived and worked in the Netherlands, Belgium, France, Germany and Switzerland and is fluent in four languages.

Index

OTHER TITLES IN THE HUMAN RESOURCE MANAGEMENT AND ORGANIZATIONAL BEHAVIOR COLLECTION

- *Conflict First Aid: How to Stop Personality Clashes and Disputes from Damaging You or Your Organization* by Nancy Radford
- *How to Manage Your Career: The Power of Mindset in Fostering Success* by Kelly Swingler
- *Deconstructing Management Maxims, Volume I: A Critical Examination of Conventional Business Wisdom* by Kevin Wayne
- *Deconstructing Management Maxims, Volume II: A Critical Examination of Conventional Business Wisdom* by Kevin Wayne
- *The Real Me: Find and Express Your Authentic Self* by Mark Eyre
- *Across the Spectrum: What Color Are You?* by Stephen Elkins-Jarrett
- *The Human Resource Professional's Guide to Change Management: Practical Tools and Techniques to Enact Meaningful and Lasting Organizational Change* by Melanie J. Peacock
- *Tough Calls: How to Move Beyond Indecision and Good Intentions* by Linda D. Henman
- *The 360 Degree CEO: Generating Profits While Leading and Living with Passion and Principles* by Lorraine A. Moore
- *The Concise Coaching Handbook: How to Coach Yourself and Others to Get Business Results* by Elizabeth Dickinson

Announcing the Business Expert Press Digital Library

Concise e-books business students need for classroom and research

This book can also be purchased in an e-book collection by your library as

- a one-time purchase,
- that is owned forever,
- allows for simultaneous readers,
- has no restrictions on printing, and
- can be downloaded as PDFs from within the library community.

Our digital library collections are a great solution to beat the rising cost of textbooks. E-books can be loaded into their course management systems or onto students' e-book readers.
The **Business Expert Press** digital libraries are very affordable, with no obligation to buy in future years. For more information, please visit **www.businessexpertpress.com/librarians**. To set up a trial in the United States, please email **sales@businessexpertpress.com**.

www.ingramcontent.com/pod-product-compliance
Lightning Source LLC
Chambersburg PA
CBHW061311220326
41599CB00026B/4831